Freedom

from

Ego

Dramas

From the Heart of Jesus, vol 6

Freedom
from
Ego
Dramas

KIM MICHAELS

MORE TO LIFE PUBLISHING

www.morepublish.com

For foreign and translation rights,

contact info@ morepublish.com

ISBN: 978-9949-518-33-3

Series ISBN: 978-9949-518-21-0

The information and insights in this book should not be considered as a form of therapy, advice, direction, diagnosis, and/or treatment of any kind. This information is not a substitute for medical, psychological, or other professional advice, counseling and care. All matters pertaining to your individual health should be supervised by a physician or appropriate health-care practitioner. No guarantee is made by the author or the publisher that the practices described in this book will yield successful results for anyone at any time. They are presented for informational purposes only, as the practice and proof rests with the individual.

For more information: *www.askrealjesus.com.*

CONTENTS

No one is more firmly trapped
than he who thinks he is free.
Ultimate freedom comes only
through oneness.

INTRODUCTION

This book is part of the *From the Heart of Jesus* series, which means the content is given through a process of direct revelation by the ascended master Jesus. For more information on how Jesus brings forth these teachings, see the first book in this series, *The Mystical Teachings of Jesus* or the websites *www.ascendedmasterlight.com* and *www.askrealjesus.com*.

This book is the third in a three-part series on the ego. It will describe the dramas created by the ego in order to distort your inner desire to make a positive difference on this planet. It will explain why so many people have been pulled into fighting for a cause by killing other people and why this has led to so many atrocities throughout history.

The first book, *Freedom From Ego Illusions*, gives a general overview of how the ego distorts your vision and how you can begin to free yourself from its illusions.

The second book, *Freedom From Ego Games*, describes the games that the ego creates in order to keep your attention focused on the ongoing human struggle and prevent you from realizing who you really are and why you are here.

Jesus recommends that you have read the first two books about the ego before reading this one.

❧

What human beings call "good" was
created in a polarity with what they call
"evil." The two are inseparable, meaning
that one can never destroy the other.

❧

1 | THE IMPORTANCE OF EGO DRAMAS

Jesus: In this book I will talk about a topic that is little known to most spiritual seekers. There are several reasons for this:

- People's egos and the false teachers of this world will do anything to prevent you from understanding what ego dramas are and how they are used to abort your growth and your expression of Christhood.

- Many people are not at a level of the spiritual path where they need to be concerned about ego dramas, as they first need to become aware of the ego's illusions and its games.

- The ascended masters have not given any teachings on this because we have not had a critical mass of people who were ready for them. This has now changed.

Why is it so important for some people to consider ego dramas? An underlying theme for my websites and for all of the books in this series is that there are currently 10,000 people in embodiment who have the potential to claim and express their Christhood in this lifetime. There are millions more who can attain a high degree of Christhood. It has therefore been my intent to give these people all the teachings and tools they need in order to manifest their highest potential.

Let me talk about two stages of spiritual growth. The first one is what we might call the general spiritual path where people are working on raising their own consciousness. The second stage is what I call the path to Christhood. During the first stage people tend to be focused on themselves, and they are often as little children who are innocently exploring what spiritual growth means and what is available in the marketplace. They are seeking to raise their own consciousness with little concern for other people or the world. Many people are reading books or following gurus that promote a more superficial form of spirituality. With superficial I mean that people have an outer path where it seems they can reach a spiritual state of consciousness without confronting the beam – the ego – in their own eyes. It is what I have called the automatic path to salvation. This path can still take people to the point where they are ready to step onto the path of Christhood.

The second stage is where people become more serious and dedicated and they realize they need to work hard and they need to change themselves. They also become more concerned about perspectives that reach beyond themselves. They often reawaken to what brought them to this planet, namely a sincere desire to improve conditions and help raise the collective consciousness.

This is a much more critical stage of the path. The high potential is that people can indeed manifest personal

Christhood and make a major contribution to raising the collective consciousness. The risk is that they can become focused on changing other people and begin to feel this justifies using means that do not respect the absoluteness of free will.

This is truly a critical distinction. If you manifest and express Christhood, you will make a real and valid contribution to raising the whole beyond the human struggle. If you go into using force, you will make severe karma for yourself and you will only contribute to dragging the whole down into another spiral of struggle.

The false teachers and the forces of anti-christ know very well how much is at stake, and that is precisely why they have defined the ego dramas. It is their ultimate weapon for diverting your path to Christhood into the false path of seeking to force people to be saved according to your vision, or rather the illusion created by the serpentine mind.

I am in no way saying this to induce fear because for those who have risen to the path of Christhood, fear is no longer the dominant emotion. Nevertheless, I am indeed saying it to promote a sense of profound realism, for there is much at stake here. The work of the ascended masters can only be fulfilled through people in embodiment. It can never be fulfilled by people who are still affected by the force-based mindset of the fallen beings. It is essential for you to come to see through this force-based mindset and see its unreality. To this end, I offer this book.

What is an ego drama?

Let me ask you to re-read what I said in the previous book about the relationship between ego games and ego dramas:

"An ego game is directly related to you and what you do as an individual whereas an ego drama relates to what you do in relation to some greater – seemingly impersonal – consideration. We might say that an ego game is what people normally see as egotistical behavior, namely what revolves around your personal desires or needs. An ego drama goes beyond your personal level and relates to a greater cause. A drama is something you pretend to do for others or even for God, yet it is simply a camouflaged offspring of the ego. An ego game is often obvious selfish behavior whereas an ego drama is selfish behavior camouflaged as unselfish behavior. An ego game is what you do in relation to other people who are also focused on themselves. An ego drama is what you do in relation to a greater cause, even to God or to other people who are also pretending that their selfish behavior serves an altruistic cause."

Truly, this is the essential point. Did I not say, those many years ago when I walked the earth in a physical body:

> But I say unto you, That ye resist not evil: but whoso-ever shall smite thee on thy right cheek, turn to him the other also. (Matthew 5:38-40)

Does this not imply a total and uncompromising respect for free will? Does it not imply that the forces of anti-christ have always sought to drag you into a struggle against them by violating your free will? They will attack you again and again and their sole purpose is to get you to react to them and to engage in a struggle against them. They know that when you resist evil, you will never manifest Christhood, for all of your energies and attention will be fed into the downward spiral of the struggle they have generated on this planet.

Just look at how many people around the world, such as in the Middle East, who are feeding their energies into struggling against other groups of people. They are feeding the fallen beings and enabling them to continue an existence. By using their free will to engage in this struggle, they also prevent the judgment of the fallen beings so that the ascended masters cannot remove them from this planet.

It is a basic fact that by resisting evil you only reinforce evil. How do you avoid resisting evil? By always turning the other cheek with complete non-attachment. How can you turn the other cheek? Only by having an uncompromising respect for free will—your own and that of others.

When the fallen beings attack you, you respect that God has given them free will. On planet earth, there is nothing that prevents them from attacking you physically. Yet you also realize the truth behind my words:

> And fear not them which kill the body, but are not able
> to kill the soul: but rather fear him which is able to
> destroy both soul and body in hell. (Matthew 10:27-29)

The fallen beings do have the power to kill your physical body, but they have no power to kill your soul. This truly means that they have no power to influence how you choose to react to them. You have – and must claim in order to walk the path of Christhood – complete mastery over your mind. "He who can destroy the soul" is actually yourself, the Conscious You. You can drag it into your own private hell of struggling against something in this world until the friction gets hotter and hotter and ends up burning the soul and its structure.

The strategy of the fallen beings

As we explain in greater depth in *Healing Mother Earth*, there are two groups of fallen beings on earth. There are those who will directly and openly violate you and seek to drag you into opposing them. The people who are ready to start the path of Christhood have risen to a level of consciousness where it is difficult for the fallen beings to drag them into this direct struggle. The second group of fallen beings have come up with the ego dramas as a way to drag you into the struggle while thinking you are working for a higher cause. The ego dramas will imply that a certain cause is so important that it justifies measures that force the will of others. It might not be overt physical force, but it is definitely a force, often a psychic force. Any use of force is a violation of the Law of Free Will, which is the most important law for this universe.

One more thing I want to give you in this introduction. As Maitreya has explained in his book, the common conception (Based on the Book of Revelation) that the fallen beings were angels who fell in heaven is not correct. The material universe is the latest in a series of spheres. A sphere is created like your world, meaning it is yet impermanent and the beings inhabiting it have not yet ascended. As the beings in a sphere raise their consciousness individually, they raise their sphere up until the entire sphere can ascend and become part of the spiritual realm.

Before a sphere ascends, there is room for the duality consciousness, meaning lifestreams can choose to go into separation. Once a sphere ascends, there is no longer room for beings who are in duality. When a previous sphere came close to the ascension point, a number of beings were not willing to leave behind duality. These were beings who had attained high positions in their unascended sphere, yet in order to ascend, they had to give up these selves. As I said: "He who would be greatest amongst you, let him be the servant of all." I also told people to be willing to lay down their lives in order to follow Christ into the ascended state of consciousness. The reason being that a separate self cannot enter the spiritual realm.

The Law of Free Will mandates that if lifestreams go into duality, they must receive many opportunities to live out this state of consciousness until they have had enough and want to return to oneness. When a sphere ascends, the beings in duality obviously cannot ascend with it so they are given the opportunity to fall into the next sphere that is being created as the previous one ascends.

When a being falls into an unascended sphere, it does not lose the separate self it has built. You now have a situation where a new sphere has two types of beings. There are new lifestreams who have a point-like sense of self and no experience with the world. Then there are the fallen beings who have a much broader sense of self and a lot of experience with the world.

This obviously gives a certain advantage to the fallen beings because they are much more sophisticated than new lifestreams. In the beginning, the fallen beings are not allowed to interact with new lifestreams, being instead given their own planets. There are numerous planets where the innocent inhabitants never chose to go into separation. These planets have evolved without ever having fallen beings embodying on them.

The Garden of Eden

As we have said, in the distant past, a critical mass of the lifestreams evolving on earth did choose to go into separation and this is what allowed fallen beings to start embodying here (this was necessary because they had destroyed their own planets). Even then, the less experienced lifestreams were placed in a protected environment. The story of the Garden of Eden is a highly incomplete illustration of such an environment, as Maitreya explains in great depth.

The "God" in the garden was Maitreya and the serpent was the fallen beings. The critical question was whether the newer lifestreams would keep their connection to the teacher or whether they would let the fallen beings deceive them into breaking that connection. Most people who are in embodiment today have broken their conscious connection to their spiritual teachers. That is why they are so easily deceived into either opposing the fallen beings or engaging in the ego dramas.

The path to Christhood is the stage of growth where you need to reestablish your full connection to your spiritual teacher by coming to see through and rise above *all* of the temptations that the fallen beings can throw at you. This includes the ego dramas, namely their attempt to abort your Christhood by seeking to force the free will of others for a greater cause. As I have tried to explain, there is no greater cause on planet earth than allowing free will to outplay itself so that people may finally have had enough and cry out for more.

You need to carefully ponder that many of those who are ready for Christhood did originally descend to planet earth, or another planet, for the specific purpose of helping to raise it beyond the consciousness of duality and the reach of the fallen beings. It is essential to realize that you cannot fulfill this goal by destroying or defeating the fallen beings. They cannot be conquered by fighting them, which is why I told people not to resist evil and why I did not resist those who killed my body— thereby claiming mastery of my mind.

I am not thereby saying that Christed beings in the modern world will have to be killed (although that is still the case in some parts of the world). I am saying that Christed beings have to be willing to attain non-attachment to anything the fallen beings can do to them so they do not allow themselves to be dragged into engaging the fallen beings by either fighting against them or fighting with them.

Some of the fallen beings literally believe they have risen to a level of self-awareness where they rival the Creator of this world of form. They believe they are capable of judging that the Creator made a mistake by giving lifestreams free will. They believe this will cause some lifestreams to become lost, and they are actively seeking to get lifestreams to become lost in order to prove their point.

The reality is that it is only the fallen consciousness that can cause a lifestream to become lost. The fallen beings are truly saying that it is God's fault that the problem of lifestreams becoming lost exists. Yet they are the ones – through their choices – who created the problem. They are saying that the very fact that they have chosen to use their free will to force the free will of others so they become lost proves that free will is wrong. The Creator should give the fallen beings the power to force lifestreams to become saved so they do not become lost. They are saying that the Creator should put them in charge of solving the problem they have created. As if the consciousness that created a problem could ever help anyone transcend the problem.

The fallen beings have created an elaborate set of ego dramas in their attempt to get the Christed beings to engage in a scheme to force people to be saved for some greater good. As I have said, this will abort your Christhood and only serve to further the cause of the fallen beings.

If you find this confusing or overwhelming, give me some time to explain it in more depth and from different angles. It truly is a difficult point to grasp, but once you grasp it, you will have taken a decisive step on the path of Christhood.

What makes a lifestream
susceptible to the epic dramas?
It is the lifestream's personal dramas
because the epic dramas tie in
to the personal dramas and offer
an even more watertight excuse for not
looking at the beam in your own eye.

2 | WHY THE EGO IS ALWAYS "RIGHT"

I n order to give you a gentle on-ramp, let me address the point of how the ego can always project that it is right. I originally described this as an ego game that sprang from the security games. On the individual level it truly is an ego game. Yet the fallen beings have taken this game and have used it to define and justify the ego dramas, which is why it is included in this book.

Myriad spiritual seekers – as well as religious and non-religious people – have spent lifetimes on the quest of proving their egos right. They have been happily following the false path – what I called the broad way that leads to destruction – instead of finding the true path to spiritual freedom.

When you take an honest look at the world, you will notice that many people are caught in the game of proving that some thought system is the only right one and that all others are false. This game takes on many disguises, and it can indeed keep people occupied for lifetimes. Yet eventually, the real you will tire of this game and begin to wonder if there isn't something beyond the thought systems found in this world, some form of ultimate truth, ultimate reality.

At that point, you are facing the essential choice that can take you onto the path of Christhood. That choice is whether you are willing to find a higher reality or whether you will simply accept a more sophisticated version of the ego game to establish the ultimate belief system. Most people, of course, do not understand the choice they are facing. My purpose for this discourse is to clarify the choice for those who are willing to understand the deeper reality behind my statement:

> 22 Ye worship ye know not what: ...
> 23 But the hour cometh, and now is, when the true worshippers shall worship the Father in spirit and in truth: for the Father seeketh such to worship him.
> 24 God is a Spirit: and they that worship him must worship him in spirit and in truth. (John, Chapter 4)

How separation leads to idol worship

Let me ask you to conduct a simple thought experiment. When I say the word "apples," take note of what happens in your mind. Immediately, a mental image comes up, a mental image of what apples mean to you. Now imagine that I tell you that a new fruit has been discovered on a remote island. I may describe it, and based on that description, you will formulate a mental image. The difference is that you have had a direct experience of apples so your mental image of apples is at least somewhat tied to reality (taking into account that the physical senses cannot be entirely trusted). On the other hand, your mental image of the unknown fruit is not tied to reality since you have not experienced it.

This shows the fundamental problem with the ego's perception of God. The ego is born from your separation from your source, and thus the ego can never have a direct experience of God. The ego will for its entire existence be basing its concept of God on a mental image that it can never compare to reality. The ego will always seek to defend its mental image of God, which means it must prevent the Conscious You from actually experiencing God. The difference being, of course, that because the Conscious You is an extension of the Creator's Being, the Conscious You can actually have an experience of God.

"Worshiping God in Spirit and in truth" means that you make use of the Conscious You's ability to have a direct experience of God's Being. People who are not willing to make use of this God-given ability – the key of knowledge – will be worshiping idols, and their entire approach to religion is based on a graven image of God. That is why you see so many religious people who insist that their religion is the only true belief system. Of course, you also see people who are doing the exact same thing with a political belief system or even the belief system called scientific materialism.

Understanding the origin of duality

Let us now move on to consider what should seem like a peculiar fact, namely why so many people can be absolutely convinced that their belief system is the only true one when there are so many conflicting belief systems that they cannot all be true. This should make people wonder whether perhaps all of them are out of touch with ultimate reality.

Let me make an absolute statement. Any belief system that has ever existed or that could ever exist on earth will give an incomplete description of God. Why is this so? Because the

Creator is beyond its creation, is beyond the totality of the material universe. No belief system could ever give an accurate or complete description of God. It is like trying to describe the sun by looking only at the moon.

The subtle difference is that because the ego is separated from God, it cannot have a direct experience of God's Being. The ego thinks God can be reduced to a description, to a mental image—which then inevitably becomes a graven image. The Conscious You can indeed have a direct experience of God's Being, and when you have this experience, you will know that God could never be described by any belief system. God can only be experienced, and as soon as you try to put words on the experience, you degrade it.

To the ego, God is not a real, Living Presence. God is a concept, a mental image. The Conscious You can experience God as a Living Being that is right here whereas the ego can only see God as a remote, conceptual being. As I said with my analogy of apples and the unknown fruit, the ego can never compare its mental image of God to reality, meaning it can never overcome its idol worship. It is up to the Conscious You to extricate itself from your ego's graven images of God. In order to do that, you need to understand how the ego expresses its insatiable desire for security in creating an infallible belief system.

The concept I will give you next might be difficult for you to grasp—if you have not yet had a direct experience of God's Being. It is still valuable for you to have this concept in your mind. It is actually not entirely correct to say that the Conscious You can have an experience of God's Being. The reason is that using the word "experience" often makes people think of experiences they have in their normal state of awareness. For example, you may go to the beach and watch a beautiful sunset, but you are aware that you are a separate observer watching the scenery from a distance. This "observing from a distance" is precisely how the ego thinks of God and thinks of the concept of experiencing God—and everything else for that matter. It thinks you have to experience God as the remote being in the sky. In reality, you will never experience God as long as you look for him outside yourself, which is why I told you that the kingdom of God is within you.

In order to experience God's Being, you have to be willing to stop seeing yourself as a separate being – at least for a moment – and instead come to experience your oneness with God. You can experience God only through what some of my early followers called "gnosis," which means a oneness between the knower and the known. The normal separation between the object and the observer is set aside and the observer becomes one with the object being observed. As a side note, this is possible because everything has consciousness. The Conscious You can experience oneness with the consciousness of any object, even a rock.

The ego can never experience Gnosis, for if it did, it would instantly cease to exist. Gnosis is oneness, and in oneness there is no room for separation, meaning that there is no room for opposing viewpoints. Because the ego was born from separation, its world view does indeed have room for opposing polarities. The ego can never escape the form of thinking that incorporates at least two polarities. Why is that so?

I have said that in God's reality there is only oneness. How can you separate yourself from oneness? You can do so only by creating a distance, which can be done only when there are two opposing polarities that are seen as being separated by space—for in oneness there is no space for distance. Only when there is distance, is there room for the illusion that you are separated from oneness and can have an existence outside of oneness, even being able to hide something from God, as Adam and Eve supposedly hid from God in the Garden.

Why are people so sure they are right?

How does this allow the ego to believe it is always right? When you create two opposing polarities, you have created a dualistic system, a dualistic world view. The ego will then impose a value judgment upon the system, defining one polarity as good, right or true and the other as evil, wrong or false. If you belong to the good polarity, you are always right compared to the people in the opposing polarity. This means you can now ignore, refute or deny any evidence or viewpoints that do not conform to your belief system. If you dismiss all contrary evidence, you can prove any point.

Most people tend to believe that if there is a conflict between two belief systems, one must be right and the other wrong. The reality is that people on both sides of a dualistic debate are out of touch with God because they are all separated from the reality of God, which is oneness. The ego can never see this, and as long as people's conscious selves cannot see through the dualistic logic, they cannot see it either. They are stuck in playing the ego game of seeking to prove that their side is right, constantly being challenged by those in the other polarity who, although they are obviously wrong, still insist that they are right.

What is the mechanism that allows people to be so convinced that they are right? When you are experiencing oneness, you are not having a mental image of God's reality. You experience oneness, and you clearly experience that everything within the Sphere of Oneness is real whereas everything outside that sphere is unreal. You also experience that only oneness exists, which means that what is outside oneness only has a temporary existence in the minds of beings caught in duality.

When you experience oneness – the Christ consciousness – you have no mental image and no value judgment. You distinguish only between what is real and what is unreal, *not* what is good or evil, true or false, right or wrong. When you separate yourself from this oneness, you become blinded by the veil of duality, which hides oneness. Instead, everything you see is based on a dualistic view in which there are two polarities. (As a side note, a person in Christ consciousness still creates mental images of what he or she wants to co-create. Yet such a person does not mistake mental images for reality.)

The ego was born from separation, and it is incapable of seeing beyond it or even questioning it. The statements I have just made about oneness cannot be grasped by the ego, which will struggle to fit them into its dualistic world view. Likewise, when the Conscious You has forgotten its origin, it too does not think to look beyond or question the dualistic world view—although it is capable of doing so.

People blinded by duality do not question the basic world view that everything can be defined based on two opposing polarities, such as good and evil. They uncritically accept the dualistic world view. They unknowingly accept the basic concept of this world view, namely that there is a division between right and wrong, true and false, good and evil. They also accept that this division is real in an ultimate sense, such as being defined by God. They fail to see that this division is defined by the dualistic system itself and has no reality outside the system.

The Christ mind sees everything in terms of what is real and unreal based on a direct experience of oneness. The mind of anti-christ sees everything in terms of right and wrong—the difference being that because it has no experience of oneness, its definition of right and wrong is based on a mental image. In the dualistic mind, right is defined in relation to – is defined as the opposite of – wrong. Yet both right and wrong are defined by the dualistic mind and have no connection to the reality of oneness. They are both graven images.

In the Christ mind, reality is not defined in relation to or in opposition to unreality. Oneness simply *is*, and it does not have, nor does it need, an opposite. In oneness there can be no opposites. Because of free will, it must be possible to step outside of oneness, and this can be done only by stepping into duality.

When you do step behind the veil of duality, you suddenly see everything as being on a relative scale with an opposing polarity at each end. This means that any dualistic thought system is based on a mental image of the world not on reality itself. This mental image is created by defining two opposites, such as God and the devil.

When a dualistic thought system is defined, it is of necessity based on an assumption, what is often called an "axiom" in logic. This is so because duality cannot experience oneness, and thus it must make an assumption about what is real and unreal. The assumption must of necessity be limited because it is separated from reality, from oneness! The assumption is based on a mental image that is disconnected from reality and can never be compared to reality—by the ego.

An axiom is a statement or premise that is thought to be self-evident or universally true, meaning it does not need to be proven or questioned. Once people have accepted a dualistic thought system, they rarely question the basic assumption upon which it is based. They accept it as universally true, and that is why they are so absolutely convinced that their thought system is the only right one and has ultimate authority.

The fallen beings define an axiom and define that it is an absolute truth. They then build a thought system upon that "truth," meaning that the thought system must of necessity be true. As long as you do not question the basic axiom, you will be absolutely convinced that your system is superior to any other. You will have the perfect excuse for ignoring conflicting views. You might even feel justified in seeking to destroy such ideas or the people who promote them. The excuse is, of course, that since your thought system is based on an infallible truth, any opposing views must – per definition – be false.

Examples of infallible belief systems

Let us look at a couple of examples. Fundamentalist Christianity is based on an axiom which states that the Bible is the infallible word of God, meaning that it has the highest possible authority. Anything conflicting or going beyond the Bible must be false. Another axiom is that the Bible should be "interpreted" literally (of course, the words "literal" and "interpretation" are contradictory), meaning that a fundamentalist church will claim that its particular "literal" interpretation of the Bible is the only true one. All conflicting interpretations must therefore be of the devil, which means fundamentalists have the perfect excuse for ignoring them. Of course, they fail to see that they are using the exact same logic that the scribes and Pharisees used against me when I stood before them in the flesh.

Another example is materialistic philosophy. It holds as an axiom that science – for example through the theory of evolution – has proven that there is nothing beyond the material universe, thus there is no God. Again, such people have the perfect excuse for ignoring any contradictory evidence – even when produced by science itself – since it is just superstition or the subjectivity of the mind.

You also have political thought systems, such as the Marxist belief that the driving force in society is the struggle between the ruling class and the workers. Again, any conflicting system must be false, and this leads to the struggle between capitalism and communism. Of course, capitalism is also a dualistic thought system based on the axiom that capitalism represents free enterprise, as opposed to a communist system with state ownership and control. Obviously, capitalism is simply another elitist system (as is communism) and thus has nothing whatsoever to do with freedom.

All of these systems cause people to accept the underlying axiom as something that should never be questioned. This means that the systems form closed boxes, and once people accept the underlying axiom, they can remain trapped indefinitely—unless they dare to question the unquestionable.

Any dualistic thought system has the perfect way to prevent people from questioning its axioms. That way is to engage people in the dualistic struggle against the enemies of the system. This can keep people's minds so preoccupied that they never actually get around to questioning the underlying assumption of their own system or of duality itself.

Any thought system in this world is based on an axiom, an assumption, a mental image. Such a system may still help you make progress by expanding your understanding, as many spiritual thought systems can do. Yet any such system sets limits for how far you can go in your quest for ultimate truth—for in order to remain within the system, you cannot question its basic axioms. You will not go beyond those limits until you are willing to question the basic assumptions upon which the system is built. This is the difference between a religious person – who never questions the basic tenets of his or her religion – and a mystic who accepts no limits for the mind.

The "advantage" of a dualistic system

Why do people accept these dualistic thought systems? They do so because the systems offer some very clear advantages—

that is, advantages for people who are trapped in duality. In the previous book, I talked about the ego's need for security, and it should be obvious that this need is cleverly filled by a dualistic thought system. The system promises that its members are superior to all other people, and the egos of the members can feel secure. For example, a fundamentalist Christian system promises that its members are the only ones who will go to heaven whereas all others will burn in hell—for all eternity.

There is also a more subtle advantage. When you accept an absolute thought system, you can no longer be proven wrong—and the ego hates nothing more than being proven wrong. You can feel secure in knowing that no matter what arguments other people come up with, you will ultimately be proven right. You can easily brush aside or ignore anything that conflicts your beliefs.

This means that you can avoid looking at the beam in your own eye, for since you are already right or superior, it can only be other people who have a problem—not you. Just look at how many fundamentalist Christians feel they are my true followers and feel they can safely ignore the beam in their own eye—and instead focus on the splinters in the eyes of other people.

There is an even more subtle advantage. Once you accept an infallible belief system, you can basically stop thinking about the more difficult questions of life. This makes your ego feel very secure and comfortable because on a surface level it can never be proven wrong by anything outside yourself. The real "advantage" is that the ego can feel it has the Conscious You under its control. As long as you are not using your ability to step outside your current mental box, there is no risk that you will question the reality of your ego. You are truly trapped and your growth has come to a complete stop.

Your choice

What is the basic choice you have to make as a result of reading this discourse? You have to decide whether you want to be right with God or whether you want to be "right" in a dualistic world. Do you want to experience God's ultimate reality, or do you want to remain in the dualistic world where you can always be proven right in opposition to something that is wrong?

If you want to be right with God – which ultimately means being in oneness – how do you get started? You need to start by taking an honest look at your belief system, your world view. You need to consider the axioms – the underlying assumptions – upon which your world view is based. You need to systematically – not all at once, but one at a time – question your axioms.

This will make your ego very uncomfortable because it will feel this is the ultimate threat to its control over you and its very survival. You should not be surprised that your ego will do everything it can to prevent you from starting or completing the process. What is its primary weapon? It is the argument that there must be something in your world view that is true—there must be something you can trust, something you can rely upon.

This argument may take any number of forms, but here is one: "Come on, now, how can this 'Jesus' say that everything you believe is wrong? You have been a student of the ascended masters for decades. You have studied all these teachings that were given directly by the ascended masters, and surely those teachings couldn't be all wrong. The real Jesus would never say something like that!"

Your ego can turn any spiritual teaching into a closed mental box, into an absolutist belief system that supports its quest for security. Many of the people who have been following the spiritual path the longest are precisely the ones who have allowed their egos to use spiritual teachings to build a sense of security—without seeing what was happening. How can you tell? If you sense any uncomfortability toward questioning your basic beliefs about life, then that uncomfortability can only come from your ego.

I am not actually saying that everything you know or believe is wrong. I am only saying that if you truly want to make progress on the *real* path to Christhood, you have to be willing to question any aspect of your world view. It is what you are not willing to question that will inevitably keep you from reaching the ultimate goal of the path.

What is that goal? It is the complete oneness with God's reality. What happens when you are in that oneness? You no longer need any thought systems. When you have a direct experience of oneness, why would you need a mental image of anything?

You can still use an outer teaching as a way to communicate with other people. Take note that I am not here saying that spiritual teachings are worthless. They are – at their best – tools for communicating an understanding that can help people progress toward a direct experience of oneness. The problem is that far too many spiritual seekers fall prey to the ego game of using a spiritual teaching to build the ego's sense of security, its sense of always being right.

The spiritual teaching that was meant to liberate them from duality now becomes an extremely efficient tool for keeping them trapped in duality. There are no people who are more firmly trapped in duality than those who have used a dualistic system to convince themselves that they are already saved. No one is more firmly trapped than he who thinks he is free. Ultimate freedom comes only through oneness.

Those who have ears had better hear, for I speak from that oneness, and I seek to bridge the gap between separation and oneness. Your Conscious You has ears to hear—if you will stop listening to the subtle temptations of the ego and admit that even if every person on earth thinks you are right, you are not right with God until you are one with God. In oneness there is no right or wrong. Oneness is all there *is*.

3 | THE UNREALITY OF THE EPIC STRUGGLE

We will now take a closer look at the epic struggle. This struggle is the single-most successful device created by the forces of anti-christ to keep human beings – and other self-aware beings – trapped in the mind of duality, thereby feeding their light to the forces of anti-christ. This light enables them to survive, even though they have long ago been cut off from receiving spiritual light directly.

The key to understanding the epic struggle is my teachings that God is undivided and indivisible. God is the Infinite, and that which is infinite is everywhere, meaning that it cannot be divided into parts that are separated by distance. Concepts such as division and distance simply have no meaning when you are talking about the ultimate God. As a side note, this means that any God who favors one group of people over all others, such as the ancient Israelites, can only be a dualistic god.

The Creator has allowed its own Being to be manifest as the Ma-ter Light out of which everything in the world of form has been given form. The Creator's Being is embedded within everything. The Creator has also allowed the creation of self-aware beings with free will. These beings are meant to serve as co-creators who bring about the unfoldment of the world of form from within. Both the Ma-ter light and the self-aware extensions of the Creator form the Divine Feminine or the Mother aspect of God.

Understanding the two basic choices

Co-creators have two spheres within which they can exercise their co-creative abilities. One is the Sphere of Oneness in which they co-create within the framework of God's laws. This means that everything they create will raise up themselves and all life, bringing God's overall plan closer to manifestation. By exercising your free will within this sphere, you do not give up any freedom. On the contrary, as illustrated in my parable about the talents, your creative abilities are multiplied, and you actually gain greater creative freedom.

The other option is to exercise your creative abilities outside the Sphere of Oneness by acting as a separate individual. This is not possible in the spiritual realm because the vibration of the Ma-ter light that forms the spiritual realm is so high that the illusion of separateness cannot be maintained. The material universe has pockets – earth being one of them – in which the vibration of the light is so low that the illusion of separation seems plausible. The illusion can be maintained only because of the density of matter that prevents your thoughts from being instantaneously manifest. This gives the illusion of a separation between consciousness and matter and makes possible the illusion that you are a separate individual who is not linked to others through the collective consciousness.

This illusion of separation gives rise to the further illusion that you can take physical actions and escape the consequences,

meaning that you can do onto others without having others –
or the universe – do onto you. This is, of course, a complete
illusion, for no one can escape the consequences of his or her
actions. When you exercise your creative abilities in a way that
limits other parts of life – seeking to raise up the separate self –
you will diminish your creative power and limit your freedom.

When people are blinded by the illusion of separation, they
fail to see this. They can – for some time – maintain the illusion
that they are raising the separate self in comparison to other
separate selves. They can even maintain the illusion that they
gain freedom only by going against God's will—the will of the
external god of their own making.

You can *co*-create in a way that raises up all life – including yourself – or you can *de*-create in a way that diminishes all
life—again, yourself included. The first option should be the
obvious choice, but once beings are blinded by the illusion of a
separate self, it is not. The illusion that you can gain an advantage by raising up the separate self in comparison to others
becomes the "obvious" choice. Out of this illusion, the epic
struggle is born.

Why the epic struggle is pointless

Many myths portray the world as being locked in an epic struggle between two opposing forces. These myths range from
ancient mythology, such as the Iliad and the Bhagavad Gita, to
modern mythology, such as Star Wars and Lord of the Rings.
Throughout the ages, many people have looked at the world
and concluded that this portrayal is true and that there is an
epic struggle. Indeed, there *is* such a struggle—only it is not
between the true God and some entity that opposes God.

When you begin to glimpse God as infinite and formless,
you see that because that which is infinite cannot be divided,

it can have no opposite. In God, there is only oneness so how can there be a struggle? The Infinite God does not see itself as opposed by anything, meaning that there is no struggle within God's Sphere of Oneness.

How is the struggle born? You can leave oneness only by creating a sense of distance, which you do by defining two opposing polarities that will forever be separated. As soon as those two polarities are defined, the epic struggle between them is the inevitable result.

I trust that those who have studied my previous ego discourses will see that the struggle can have no reality in God. It can exist only in the minds of self-aware beings who have stepped outside the Sphere of Oneness—meaning that it is ultimately unreal. Why is it unreal?

The promise of the struggle is that there are two sides and that one represents ultimate good and the other ultimate evil. By aligning yourself with ultimate good and by fighting against the people who are aligned with evil, you – as a separate self – will gain a distinct advantage. Eventually, ultimate good will win the struggle and then all who helped destroy ultimate evil will be rewarded.

On a deeper level, this promise of a reward for a separate self is an illusion—since the separate self is an illusion. Of course, no one blinded by separation can see this. Yet even those blinded by separation can see that if the promise of a reward was false, it would be silly of them to fight for one side and *against* the other. Consider how the promise could be fulfilled? It can happen only when good finally destroys evil. On a deeper level, what human beings call "good" was created in a polarity with what they call "evil." The two are inseparable, meaning that one can never destroy the other. The only way for the epic struggle to end is if both are transcended! Good does not cancel out evil. The reality of God cancels out the illusion of the dualistic struggle.

No one blinded by separation can see this point, as such beings cannot see beyond the illusion of separation. Those who have started seeing beyond duality can see that the epic struggle is utterly pointless. It simply is not possible that good can win over evil, for "good" and "evil" are relative terms that cannot exist independently of each other. They were created together and can only be "erased" together.

You might say that ultimate good can win, but even that is an incorrect use of words. Ultimate good – the indivisible God – is not engaged in any struggle, for it recognizes no division— his eyes behold no iniquity. The ultimate God is not trying to defeat the devil, for God recognizes the unreality of the devil and thus sees no need to engage him in any way. The devil is not a threat to the Creator—the devil is simply irrelevant.

The epic struggle is a grand illusion that has the effect of sucking people into an activity that eats up their attention and energy without having the potential of giving them what they seek. Even spiritual seekers can be sucked into this struggle by thinking they are fighting for the ultimate cause, fighting for God's cause. Even ascended master students have had their attention consumed by the struggle.

This brings us to an interesting point, for some will say that the ascended masters have encouraged people to engage in the struggle by decreeing "against" certain dark forces and calling forth their judgment. In order to understand this, you need to recognize that we of the ascended masters have only one goal and that is to raise the consciousness of all people. We will therefore have to meet people at the level of consciousness where they are at, and then give them teachings that take them up from there. Until recently, very few people on this planet have been ready for the non-dualistic teachings we are releasing today.

In the past, we had to adapt to what people could grasp, and the fact is that even the epic struggle can be used to promote spiritual progress. One of the greatest enemies of progress is that people become comfortable in a certain lifestyle and simply want to enjoy life in the material realm. Throughout the ages, the epic struggle has indeed had the effect of pulling people out of that comfortability and "forcing" them to increase their skills in order to "defeat" the enemy—as for example seen in martial arts.

Even though the struggle is an illusion, it can still be used to promote growth. The downside, of course, is that once people become warriors, they can become stuck in that role for many lifetimes before they finally move on to become sages, seeking peace through the mind rather than seeking it through victory in war.

It has always been our hope that those who are direct students of the ascended masters would eventually rise above the struggle, as we have indeed given veiled teachings on this in the past—for those who have eyes to read between the lines. For those who have not been willing to see this, we have had no other option than to push people's buttons in order to intensify the sense of struggle until people finally have enough. How long can you be in the mindset of fighting a war? Even the second world war lasted only five years, but some students have been fighting their own private, spiritual war against evil for decades. Their egos are laughing all the way to the bank where they cash in the light that people misqualify through the struggle.

The illusion of a separate salvation

Once people engage in the epic struggle, they inevitably become more and more focused on themselves—as a distinct group set apart from all other people. An extreme example of this is the idea that a small tribe in the Middle East was – and is – God's chosen people and will be favored above all others. There are many more examples of this, for example that the members of a small fundamentalist church are the only ones who will be saved by my return, or the idea that the members of an ascended master organization are more advanced than anyone else on the planet.

What is wrong with this idea? The plan of God is for the raising up of all life until the entire sphere of the material universe ascends and becomes a part of the spiritual realm. This does entail that individual people raise their consciousness and thereby pull up the collective consciousness. Raising your individual consciousness will eventually lead to Christ consciousness. When you do attain this consciousness, you rise above the illusions of the ego whereby you see the oneness of all life. God is seeking to raise up all life because to God all life is part of the One Greater Self—the only self that exists.

When you attain Christ consciousness, you see that "inasmuch as ye have done it unto the least of these my little ones, ye have done it unto me." You see through the lie of a separate salvation for one group or even yourself. You see the reality of the oneness of life and your focus shifts from the – ego-based – drive to raise up yourself to the true desire to raise up yourself only as a way to raise the All. As I said:

And I, if I be lifted up from the earth, will draw all men unto me. (John 12:32)

Those who think they are working for the salvation of a narrow group are still caught in the epic struggle. By the very mindset of separating people into those who will be saved and those who will not – based on outer characteristics and not individual choice – they are reinforcing the dualistic mindset that inevitably pits one group of people – as representatives of good – against another group that represents evil.

Millions of religious people are very sincere in their desire to save the world and save other people, but they are misguided in how this should be done. They think the only way is to convert everyone to their religion, based on the dualistic illusion that membership of an earthly religion will guarantee your salvation.

The only key to salvation is to raise your consciousness, and that can be attained regardless of your membership or non-membership of any earthly institution. The ascended masters do not want our present students to continue in this work. We want you to rise above duality and then – when you have removed the beam of duality from your own eye – help others do the same.

The sense of urgency

Why is the epic struggle so captivating? Why does it have the ability to suck people in so they forget everything else and become unbalanced? It is because it automatically implies a sense of urgency. If you study the techniques used in brainwashing – or even in sales techniques – you will see that in order to get people to make rash decisions, you have to create a sense of urgency that puts people under pressure. What greater urgency could there be than the imminent end of the world where Jesus will return and judge all those who are not members of your religion?

Consider some of the other myriad variations over the basic theme of the epic struggle. Look at how many times people have been sucked into thinking that they have to engage in violent actions in order to overcome some form of evil before an epic calamity takes place. What greater urgency can there be than thinking the future of the entire universe, or of God's plan for that universe, depends on the actions of a small group of people on earth? Even thinking global warming will wipe out all life is a version of the epic struggle.

This makes the egos of such people feel an ultimate sense of importance—something the ego craves as part of its quest for security. Surely, those who respond to the need to save the universe will receive some ultimate reward when evil is finally conquered.

This sense of urgency can have the effect of pulling people out of indifference and getting them to strive to excel. Even though this can have a positive effect of getting people to engage in the path of personal growth, it is only meant to be a stage on the path. You are meant to grow out of the sense of urgency so that you naturally continue your growth but now do it with a sense of inner peace.

We of the ascended masters know that as long as people are focused on enjoying material pleasures, or are otherwise indifferent to rising above the mass consciousness, they cannot grow spiritually. We will indeed use the sense of urgency to get people to start the spiritual path. Yet once people are locked in to the path, we have no desire to see them continue in the sense of urgency, thinking the world will end in the near future. Obviously, there are cycles in the journey of this planet. There are indeed times when an extraordinary effort is needed.

Even in those times, we would much prefer that our students lock in to the deeper reality that the world will not end but will continue to provide a platform for the growth of self-aware beings. The further you go on the path to Christhood, the more the sense of urgency should diminish and give way to a deep inner peace, the peace that passes understanding because it is beyond this world. It is the peace of knowing who you are—an immortal spiritual being who is only temporarily participating in the drama called "Life on earth." This does not cause you to become indifferent; it only causes you to act from peace rather than fear.

4 | HOW THE EPIC STRUGGLE IS JUSTIFIED

The most dangerous effect of the epic struggle is that it serves as the perfect "machine" for allowing the ego to justify doing what it wants to do—namely raise itself up by putting others down. Seeing this should not require much thought. Just look at how the sense of an epic struggle makes it justifiable to do virtually anything to "save the universe from destruction." When you add to that the sense of urgency, you will see how people can be made to do things that they know are wrong while being absolutely convinced that they are necessary in order to bring about a greater good or avoid a greater evil.

The most dangerous effect of the epic struggle is that it leads to the consciousness that "the ends can justify the means." This is the very consciousness that is responsible for the vast majority of atrocities seen in known history and beyond. When the "end" is believed to be serious enough, it follows that any means that are believed to be necessary for achieving that end are automatically justifiable. Normal moral or ethical concerns simply do not apply. What is actually happening in this process?

Although most people are blinded by the duality consciousness, most are not so blinded that they have lost all sense of a greater reality. The Conscious You can never totally forget its origin, and it cannot completely lose an innate sense that doing certain things is not in your own best interest. The only way your ego can get you to do something that your Conscious You knows is non-constructive is to find a way to neutralize your inner sense of reality.

The primary tool for doing this is, of course, the epic struggle. There is a power elite of fallen beings who are seeking to control planet earth and its inhabitants. These beings have – as a result of their own choices – cut themselves off from being able to receive light directly from the spiritual realm. Their continued existence is dependent upon stealing light from beings who have not yet lost that connection. This can be done only by getting people to misqualify the pure spiritual energy they receive from above, which is best done by tricking people into engaging in any self-centered activity. In order to achieve this, these forces of anti-christ – what I called the "prince of this world" – have created elaborate schemes that build on the epic struggle. For examples of this, take a look at history and see how many schemes have been used to override the most basic sense of right and wrong, namely the inner knowing that it is wrong to kill another human being.

This is truly the most basic of all moral imperatives, for the Conscious You knows that it has no right to take the life of another human being—it has no right to so drastically violate the free will of another being. I realize most people will immediately seek to qualify this by referring to self-defense, but the self that is defended by killing another human being is the separate self, and the act of defending it only reinforces the sense of separation. Because this is a crucial point, let us take a closer look.

Understanding the command "Thou shallt not kill"

When you look at history, it is clear that the members of the three monotheistic religions, Judaism, Christianity and Islam, have engaged in conflicts that killed millions of people. The people doing this killing were deeply religious people who honored the Old Testament, the center of which is the Ten Commandments, one of which states: "Thou shallt not kill."

This commandment is but an outer reminder of the innate sense that you have no right to kill another human being. How can the members of these religions be made to override both the inner command of their own beings and the outer command of their religion?

When you look at the text of the Ten Commandments, you will see that it is unconditional. The commandments do not specify any conditions under which it becomes acceptable to kill. I know that you can quickly point to other passages in the Old Testament in which God supposedly commands the Israelites to kill other people, but there is a contrast between the unconditional nature of the Ten Commandments and the rest of the Old Testament. What is happening here?

The entire story of the Israelites being imprisoned by Pharaoh is a metaphor for the enslavement of the spiritual people of earth by the elite of fallen beings trapped in the consciousness of anti-christ. "Egypt" is a symbol for the duality consciousness, as opposed to "Israel" – *Is real* – which symbolizes the state of oneness with your source.

The escape from Egypt is a symbol for a cycle in earth's history where greater numbers of people started to question their overlords. We of the ascended masters were allowed to send various teachers to represent the Christ consciousness and lead people out of the duality of "Egypt" and toward the promised land of oneness.

Moses ascending the mountain represents that such a leader goes to get a new covenant that can guide the people in their newfound freedom. The withdrawal of the teacher was also a test to see whether the people would rise to use their inner discernment or would simply look for another overlord to tell them what to do. The people cannot be free from a tyrant until they are willing to take responsibility for themselves. Moses did originally get a higher covenant, but when he returned and saw that in his absence the people had sunk right back into the duality consciousness instead of rising to the occasion, he smashed it in anger (which was a mistake on his part that cost him his ascension in that lifetime).

Moses had to go back and get a covenant adapted to the lower consciousness of a particular group of people, meaning that the original covenant was withheld for a time. That is why the Ten Commandments are such direct statements of "do this" and "don't do that," instead of a higher teaching.

As a side note, the original covenant was then given by me in my embodiment as Jesus. You will see the seeds of non-duality between the lines of my teaching, as I have explained throughout my books and website. You will also see that I had to pass the test of not reacting with anger no matter how the people responded to my ministry. I had to pass the ultimate test of letting them humiliate and kill me without responding with anger. In doing so, I cemented the new covenant and made it a permanent part of the collective consciousness. Since then, people have had a greater opportunity to embody the Christ consciousness on earth—an opportunity that was – in practicality, not in theory – out of reach before.

The new covenant – the Christ covenant – is one of the people using their innate ability – the key of knowledge – to discern between what is God's reality and what is an unreality created by the duality consciousness. The most important effect of this is that people use their discernment to see through the many subtle disguises of the epic struggle and the consciousness that the ends can justify the means.

The conclusion being, of course, that the ends can *never* justify the means. This can be understood only when you know the reality of which kind of "end" God is looking for. As I have explained, the goal of God is to raise up *all* life. This cannot be achieved by using means that put down – or kill – one part of life while raising up another. Killing is never justified in the greater cause of raising up the All, which is precisely why I told people not to resist evil but to turn the other cheek. Turning the other cheek is the only way to avoid being pulled into the dualistic struggle.

The ego and the false teachers of anti-christ have come up with myriad schemes for overriding the Conscious You's inner sense of reality. They seek to get you to ignore, override or analyze away your inner knowing so you fall prey to the belief that in this particular case it is justifiable to do what you know to be unacceptable.

Letting something in this world override your inner sense of reality is never justified and will never contribute to God's cause of raising up the All. For true students of Christ, this entire consciousness must be unmasked and abandoned, which means you must begin by looking for this beam in your own eye.

The epic struggle in your personal life?

The epic struggle has a number of very serious effects on a world scale, most notably in serving as the "perfect" justification for war, genocide, discrimination, racial tension and so forth. My concern in this context is to show you that the epic struggle has a very serious effect on the individual level, an effect that can abort your personal growth toward Christhood. What is that effect? Take a look at this statement of mine:

> 3 And why beholdest thou the mote that is in thy brother's eye, but considerest not the beam that is in thine own eye?
> 4 Or how wilt thou say to thy brother, Let me pull out the mote out of thine eye; and, behold, a beam is in thine own eye?
> 5 Thou hypocrite, first cast out the beam out of thine own eye; and then shalt thou see clearly to cast out the mote out of thy brother's eye.
> (Matthew, Chapter 7)

The ego, of course, never wants to take responsibility for anything (as described in the previous book) so it wants to point the finger at someone else. The epic struggle gives the perfect justification for turning other people into scapegoats and saying that they are the ones creating all of the problems on this planet or in your personal life. You don't have to change, for they are the ones with the problem. As long as you believe in this – and stay engaged in the struggle with other people – your ego can feel secure. How can you possibly unmask your own ego as long as you are always looking outside yourself? Can you see this ego game at work in the way you interact with or view other people, from your spouse and family to other groups of people?

Many otherwise sincere spiritual seekers – including many who call themselves ascended master students – are still trapped in a subtle form of this ego game. They think they are being spiritual and doing something important to save the world, but in reality, they have used their own version of the epic struggle as an excuse for not doing the only thing that can truly save the world, namely that they attain the Christ consciousness.

What will save the world – by raising the collective consciousness of humankind – is that a critical mass of people attain personal Christhood. For you to attain that, you must stop looking outside yourself and be willing to look for the elements of duality in your own consciousness.

The equation is very simple. You may be able to see all kinds of faults in other people, and they may indeed be valid faults. Yet the faults or virtues of other people have absolutely no impact on your personal growth toward Christhood. Even if you could see through every single human fault in other people, it would not take you one step closer to Christhood. What will take you closer to Christhood is that you see an element of duality in your own mind and then decide to rise above it.

You will not grow as long as you are looking outside yourself and refuse to look in the mirror. The epic struggle is your ego's perfect diversionary mechanism for getting you to always look for the faults of other people and neglect looking at yourself. Add to this the sense of urgency that we have to save the planet before a certain deadline, and you have the "perfect storm" that keeps people so busy with external activities that they never have the attention left over for looking within. Where did I say that the kingdom of God is to be found? Why do even ascended master students keep believing that they can find it somewhere else?

The only way to save the world is to help all people rise above the illusion of separation and the lies of duality. This cannot be done by defeating other people but only by you seeing beyond duality and then helping others do the same. Oneness is the only way to end separation and oneness must begin with you seeing oneness with your own higher being and then oneness with all life. There is no other way.

Many sincere and well-meaning people have used the teachings of the ascended masters – and the sense of urgency of having to save the world for Saint Germain – as an excuse for not healing their own psychological wounds. They now have an excuse for not making use of available techniques for psychological healing, including therapy. I have given both inner and outer direction for all spiritual students to work on healing their psychological wounds and hang-ups. Have you reasoned that because this is such a critical time, you do not have time to work on yourself, for you have to do this or that outer activity to save the world—and then you can worry about saving yourself?

This reasoning can come from only one source, namely your ego. There are two major things wrong with it. One is that the only way to save the world is to raise people to Christhood, for only this will pull up the collective consciousness. The other thing is that I am not concerned about saving the world—I am only concerned about saving individual beings, for that is the very purpose for the existence of the world. Trying to save the world before saving yourself is putting the cart before the horse.

If you are finally ready to neutralize your ego's lies and look for the beam in your own eye, I suggest available forms of psychological healing, all of our books and tools and my *Course in Christhood*.

5 | THE ORIGIN OF PERSONAL DRAMAS

I have said that there is a blurred line between ego games and ego dramas. I have also said that when the fallen beings started to embody on this planet, they took the ego games already created by the people on earth and they gave them a twist so that they became ego dramas. Of course, they also added some dramas that no people on earth had thought about or could have thought about.

As an example, let me refer to what I said about competition games, namely that people who go into separation can begin to see themselves as being in competition with other people. They desire to be superior to others by doing better than them in sport, business or as a warrior.

The ego game of competition is in a sense straightforward and honest. It is a matter of improving yourself so you can do better than others in your chosen field. In its pure form, this is all focused on you and improving your own abilities. Quite frankly, this can serve the cause of expanding your self-awareness, as proven by some martial arts practitioners who have added a spiritual dimension to being a warrior. Once you transcend the need to compete against or fight others, you will have expanded your sense of self and your awareness of how the material universe works, even how your mind can use the body and direct energy.

Take note that in its pure form, competition is based on a strict honor code. There are certain things you don't do because that would take away your honor, your self-esteem. For example, you don't do anything to ruin your competitors' ability to compete, you don't cheat and you don't use deceptive or violent means to take your competitors out of the competition. There is an invisible line that you simply do not cross because you can see no justification for doing so.

We can say that in a competition game, there are heroes but no villains. Sometimes you are the hero and sometimes it is someone else, but everyone follows the honor code. What can turn a friendly competition game into an unfriendly competition drama is the fallen beings who add the twist that the game has a "greater purpose" and a villain who opposes that purpose.

For example, there might be a power play between nations, such as seen during the Cold War between the Soviet Union and the West. It isn't enough to win based on ability alone because winning demonstrates the superiority of your political system, which is the ultimate higher purpose. It now becomes acceptable, even desirable, to use any means in order to give your nation more gold medals. In that context, using experimental steroids to boost the abilities of your young athletes becomes a justifiable necessity, and the long-term effects on the health of the athletes is simply not a concern for those directing the drama.

Take note that this overall concern that the state or the system is more important than the individual is very much a mentality that the fallen beings brought to this planet. It is not something that the original inhabitants of the earth came up with on their own. The original people had competition games, but it was the fallen beings who taught them how to create the ultimate competition game, namely war.

What is the underlying mentality here? Why didn't human beings have war games? Because they had a certain kinship with each other and it was difficult for them to justify killing each other. The fallen beings had – and have – no reverence for life in general, but they especially have no sense of kinship with the beings on earth. On the contrary, they look down upon them as being far below them and much less sophisticated. Indeed, when it comes to controlling or destroying others, human beings are far less "sophisticated" than the fallen beings.

Seeing your own mental box

Having said what I said above, I need to add a word of caution. It is very tempting to say that this earth wasn't too bad until the fallen beings came here and they were the ones that really perverted everything. Saying this is actually not far from reality. Yet there is an essential distinction between seeing the reality of what the fallen beings have done and then appointing them as scapegoats so you don't need to look at yourself.

The essential characteristic that allows you to step onto the path of personal Christhood is your willingness to question your mental boxes. The real question is whether knowledge of a certain topic takes you closer to Christhood or further away from it. I have said that you simply cannot make it on the path of Christhood unless you recognize the existence of the fallen beings and begin to see through their deceptions. Will knowing about the fallen beings take you closer to taking full responsibility for yourself, or will it serve only to give you an excuse for not looking at the beam in your own eye? The answer, of course, depends on what you do with your knowledge about the fallen beings. Or rather, it depends on whether you are willing to see that the fallen beings could control human beings only because they took advantage of the psychology that human beings had already developed. Until you begin to see what it is in your psychology that makes you vulnerable to the deception of the fallen beings, you have not really started the path to Christhood.

The path toward Christhood is an ongoing process with many levels. Until you ascend, you will have a mental box. Your progress from any level will be determined by your willingness to question your mental box. The ego and the fallen beings will always seek to make you cling to your current mental box.

As you rise on the spiritual path, the mental boxes become more subtle and more difficult to see. Many sincere spiritual seekers have allowed their egos, their friends or the false teachers to make them believe that they have reached a level at which they no longer have or need to question any mental boxes.

Let me make an absolute statement. There is not now and there never has been any being in embodiment on earth – no matter how advanced such a one might appear or claim to be – who has had no mental box left. If you truly have no mental box, it is not possible to remain in embodiment in the current density of this planet. You will inevitably be pulled up and lose your ability to hold on to the physical body. When I was hanging on the cross and one hairsbreadth away from winning my ascension, I still had to "give up the ghost" of the last remnants of my mental box. As soon as I did indeed give it up, I drew my last breath and left the physical body behind.

Had I not been willing to entertain the possibility that I could have a mental box, what would have happened? I would not have qualified for my ascension! My body would still have died on the cross, but I would have re-embodied to outplay whatever drama I had not been willing to see and surrender.

Even if you are one decision away from qualifying for your ascension, you still have that last step to take and what might it be? It is precisely that you give up the last mental box, the last illusion based on the consciousness of separation.

Another important perspective is that the path of Christhood has several levels. As you rise to a given level, you will be able to see something that was invisible to you before. What you see at the higher level might give you an entirely different perspective on certain elements of life or the spiritual reality.

The ego and the fallen beings have set up the ego dramas precisely to prevent you from letting go of the old. How can the ascended masters help you escape this? By giving you information that challenges your current mental box. If you insist that your existing view is an absolute truth, then you will obviously have to reject what we are saying.

At the higher levels of Christhood, you begin to see that no knowledge expressed in this world is the absolute or highest truth. There is always a step higher, namely a direct experience of the Spirit of Truth. In order to have the fullness of that experience in the ascension spiral, you must be willing to give up everything you think you know right now. I do mean everything.

What you need to know about the universe

As I have already described, the world of form was created as a series of spheres. Each sphere was created out of a certain type of energy, we might say a certain density or a certain frequency spectrum. When a sphere is created, it contains only energy of a certain base vibration, or we might say it has only a certain intensity of light.

The beings who created the sphere then send self-aware extensions of themselves into the sphere. These co-creators take on "bodies" made from the energies in the sphere, which in your case on earth is your physical body (in previous spheres bodies were made of energies with far less density). The co-creators then act on the command to "multiply and have dominion," meaning they use the energies in their sphere combined with their creative talents and their ability to let light from a higher sphere flow through them. By multiplying the talents, they raise the intensity – the base vibration – of the sphere until the intensity reaches a critical level.

At that point, the entire sphere is ready to ascend and become part of the ascended realm. While this sounds very neat and simple, the actual process is, of course, far more complex. What makes it complex is that co-creators have free will. This means that while there is a blueprint, there is no pre-defined "destiny" for a given sphere. It is theoretically possible that a sphere could not increase in intensity, which means that the built-in safety mechanism (what your scientists call the second law of thermodynamics) will cause it to become increasingly dense until it self-destructs and all structures are gone. In that case, there is no longer a platform for co-creators to embody.

So far, this has not happened to any sphere, and it is – quite frankly – unlikely that a majority of the co-creators in a sphere would refuse to multiply the talents. As new spheres were created from increasingly "dense" energies, there did come a point where a number of co-creators were not ready to ascend when their sphere ascended. These lifestreams could not ascend, and while they would then descend and embody in the next sphere, their non-ascension did leave empty spaces in the matrix or mandala of their sphere. One could say that they were "lost" to the ascended sphere.

This is, of course, perfectly within the Law of Free Will, as the Creator gave complete freedom to self-aware beings, meaning that they also have the option to go against the upward pull of their sphere. The simple explanation is that the Creator does not want any being to be forced to rise in self-awareness. Within certain wide boundaries, a being has complete freedom to have any experience it wants for as long as it wants. The opportunity of a self-aware being to experience separation can go beyond the time it takes for its original sphere to ascend. If not, the concept of a "fall" would not be possible. Let us now look at how it is possible for a self-aware being *not* to ascend with its original sphere.

The origin of roles

In order to explain how a sphere progresses toward the ascension point, let me give you an illustration based on what you know from earth. It will not be completely universal because earth is in a lower sphere than previous ones but the principle will apply. As an example, let us look at Europe and let us go back to the stone age. What has been happening in Europe is that there exists an etheric blueprint for how Europe can evolve from the stone age level toward a golden age civilization.

Over time, many of the people embodying in Europe have tuned in to this blueprint and have brought society forward in a variety of ways. Some have done this with greater self-awareness and have had a clearer vision of the end goal although no one has had the full vision. Others have had less self-awareness but have still made a positive contribution. Even a peasant or factory worker can be making a positive contribution to the overall progress of society.

As society has progressed, it has gone through many phases. Gradually, it has moved toward a greater and greater collective awareness and a greater awareness of the potential to reach an end goal. What we now need to add is that the people who embody in Europe today have done so for many lifetimes.

This means that over time they have had the opportunity to embody in many different circumstances and have many different experiences by having different positions in society. We might compare this to a theater production in which the actors rotate so that each actor over time plays every role in the play. Naturally, this will increase the actors' awareness of and appreciation for the overall vision of the play.

As individual co-creators rise in self-awareness, they grasp more and more of the overall vision. This means that at the conscious level, a common vision and goal begins to emerge. People no longer see themselves as disconnected individuals. They see themselves as part of something larger, and this gives them a deeper sense of meaning, purpose and fulfillment.

We might say that the lifestreams involved with the process move from a separate or localized awareness towards a global awareness. In the beginning, they only work for individual goals, but over time they have enough of playing such roles. They gradually begin to play the roles that more directly work toward the common goal, and they find greater satisfaction in working with others on an overall vision. They move from being apart from the whole toward voluntarily and with full awareness becoming a part of the whole.

The entire purpose of the world of form is the growth in self-awareness of individual lifestreams. A lifestream must start somewhere so it starts out with a very localized sense of self-awareness, for example as a human being on earth who is only concerned about itself and its own desires, needs and wants. For a new lifestream, this is not selfish or egotistical; it is simply a natural way to start the process. As long as the lifestream gradually grows toward an expanded self-awareness – goes from a localized to global awareness – there is nothing wrong with this and it contributes to the growth of the whole. When a new lifestream starts its journey in the world of form, it has a very localized, point-like self-awareness. This is comparable in some way to a newborn baby who does not have enough awareness to choose what it wants to be when it grows up. A new co-creator does not have enough self-awareness to define how it wants to express itself in the sphere in which it has been created. It needs some experience before it can decide this consciously. In order to give it such experience, it is placed in an environment where there is a number of predefined roles.

Compare this to an unexperienced actor who could not walk right into the theater and play Hamlet. He starts out playing a simpler part and gradually takes on more complex roles as his experience with the theater and his self-awareness grows. He might even increase both until he is able to write his own plays and define his own roles.

The Creator is One—it has an indivisible self-awareness. Out of its own Being, the Creator creates self-aware extensions who do not have the global or universal self-awareness. They start out with a point-like self-awareness but have the potential to expand it until it becomes as global or universal as that of their source. How can this happen? The co-creator must continually expand its self-awareness by seeing itself as part of something greater than its sense of self.

As its vision of that "something greater" expands, it begins to grasp that it is part of the Creator's Being, eventually becoming one with the totality of the Creator's Being and thus being able to now be a self-aware Creator. This process can be completed only by moving from a localized self-awareness toward a global self-awareness. There is no other way. Only by becoming one with your Creator, can you reach the ultimate level of self-awareness. You cannot reach this with a separate self-awareness, with a self-awareness as being apart from the whole—no matter how complex or seemingly sophisticated that separate self becomes. It is quite possible that, as an ideal scenario, an entire sphere – even larger than the material universe – can progress toward the ascension point with all co-creators playing progressively more complex roles until their self-awareness is expanded to the point where they can ascend when the sphere itself ascends.

The choice of co-creators

The Creator is One Being and is indivisible. It is not possible for the Creator to create something that is separate from itself. As it creates a self-aware being with localized awareness, it creates a being who can think it is less than or apart from the whole. This being has only limited co-creative abilities. By expanding its localized sense of self, it will gain greater co-creative abilities. When it reaches the self-awareness of the Creator, it attains unlimited creative abilities.

The reason is that it is possible for a being with localized awareness to use its co-creative abilities without considering the impact it has on the whole. Its abilities are limited so that its potential to destroy is limited. As it becomes more aware of the whole, its co-creative abilities are expanded because now it is less likely to use them in destructive ways.

When a sphere is created, it is inhabited by new co-creators who see themselves as separate from each other and from the forms in their sphere (such as human beings seeing themselves separate from each other and from the planet upon which they live). This is a perspective created in the minds of co-creators. In reality, a sphere is a unit, an interconnected whole.

The entire material universe is a unit and as co-creators multiply their talents, they will increase the light intensity, which will create an upward momentum. This can be compared to a force of gravity that pulls on everything in the unit.

Compare this to the earth where everything on earth is pulled toward the gravitational center and held in place so that it can move with the whole as the earth hurtles through space at incredible speed.

This upward momentum can be called the River of Life or, in Christian terminology, the Holy Spirit. It is created as co-creators transcend their original, localized self-awareness and begin to see themselves as part of a greater whole. We might say that the Holy Spirit is the awareness or vision of an underlying whole that ties all life together into a unit. As the collective vision of that greater whole expands, the gravitational force of the Holy Spirit increases.

The effect is that it now becomes easier for co-creators to expand their self-awareness and see themselves as part of a greater whole. Those who voluntarily and consciously choose to participate in this common process experience an increased sense of purpose, meaning and fulfillment. This sense of fulfillment is far greater than what can be achieved as a localized individual who sees itself as being apart from the whole.

Taking full responsibility for yourself

We now need to recognize a very important aspect of the growth process, explained in greater detail in Maitreya's book. As I have said, a co-creator starts out by playing a predefined role in a larger unit, such as a civilization on earth. This is much like small children who play "house" in order to practice the roles they take on as adults. As a co-creator plays a variety of roles, two things happen. It gains greater experience with how its sphere works and it increases its self-awareness.

This leads toward a point where the co-creator no longer fully identifies itself with or as the role it is currently playing. A new co-creator is fully identified with its role, as you see some people on earth who are completely identified with their physical bodies. As it matures, the co-creator begins to realize it is more than its current role. Eventually, it begins to realize that it is more than any predefined role in its current environment. The co-creator is now ready to take a crucial step on the path toward God realization, namely to begin to define its own role instead of simply taking on a role defined by its spiritual teachers.

What is the crucial thing that needs to happen in the mind of the co-creator before it can take this step? It is that the co-creator must make the decision to accept full responsibility for itself, for its own growth, for what on earth might be called its own "salvation." So far, the co-creator has not had to accept this responsibility because it was playing a predefined role. Compare this to an actor who goes on stage with a certain costume and has a predefined script that tells him what to say. Now imagine that an actor is told he has to go on stage and select his own costume and with no predefined script decide what to say. You will see that this can give rise to a new level of performance anxiety.

In the first three spheres, the vast majority of co-creators went through this transition with only minimal difficulty. Starting in the fourth sphere, a relatively small number of co-creators became so concerned about the potential for making mistakes that they refused to take full responsibility and define their own roles. They attempted to go back and play one of the predefined roles. The problem was that their self-awareness had already gone beyond the level where they could identify fully with the role. In order to deal with this, they had to turn away from their spiritual teacher. In order to do that, they had to come up with some form of justification.

There are various explicit forms of justification, but the underlying mentality was that they felt forced by the teacher to take the next step and that they rebelled against having to do this. What actually happened was that the co-creator – who was asked to define its own role as part of the whole – refused to do this and instead defined its own role as being apart from the whole. The co-creator still defined its own role, only it defined it in a way that cut it off from its teacher and limited its self-awareness.

When you define a role for yourself as part of the whole, playing that role will raise your self-awareness and it will raise the whole. In order to define a role as being apart from the whole, you have to make the decision to stop your growth in self-awareness—and this decision must be justified. How can a self-aware being justify the decision to stop its growth in self-awareness (which is its reason for being)? Only by accepting the belief that it is a victim of something, namely that the whole is seeking to force it rather than seeking to help it grow.

This belief cannot come from the co-creator itself, meaning from the Conscious You. It can come only from a "self" based on the illusion of separation and this new self is what becomes the ego. The ego was born out of the Conscious You's refusal to take responsibility for defining its own role. The Conscious You is still defining its own role, but because it is denying this, it now believes that it has not defined its role but that this role has been forced upon it from without. We might say that the Conscious You has still created its own role, but it has not taken responsibility for doing so.

What is the crucial difference? It is that if the Conscious You had followed the teacher's call, it would have defined a role and it would have been aware that this was only a role. By learning from playing the role, it could at any time change or expand the role until it eventually transcended the role. When the Conscious You defines a role without taking responsibility, it thinks the role was forced upon it. It comes to identify itself with and as the role, thinking it cannot expand it or rewrite the script. It feels stuck in the role instead of seeing it as merely a learning experience. It resists learning from the role, and this means it cannot come to the point where it can transcend the role.

The spiritual teacher has uncompromising respect for free will. When the student decides to define a role based on separation, the teacher cannot pursue or force the student to accept his help. The teacher must withdraw and this is what makes the student feel it has been cast out of the Garden of Eden and that there are angels with flaming swords preventing it from coming back. In reality, it is only the student's unwillingness to take full responsibility for itself that prevents it from coming back to the circle of the teacher's guidance.

Free will and others

Here, we have a subtle point. Refusing to take full responsibility for defining its own roles is completely within the Law of Free Will. An individual co-creator has the right to do this. What an individual cannot do is to set itself apart from the whole in which it lives. A person on earth may rebel against the force of gravity but will still be moving through space along with the earth. An individual co-creator can decide that it wants to stop its own growth, but it cannot ask others to do the same. An individual can stand still but cannot expect or demand that the billions upon billions of other co-creators in its entire sphere should stand still.

Because the individual is still part of the whole, as the other co-creators expand their self-awareness, they create a stronger momentum of the Holy Spirit that will pull on the individual who stands still. The gravitational pull of the collective momentum of the Holy Spirit creates a pull on the individual, which means it becomes a struggle to uphold and justify the individual's role as being apart from the whole and the process of growth. This tension between the individual and the whole is what creates a drama in the mind of the individual.

The drama is created because as the Holy Spirit increases, it becomes increasingly difficult for the individual to justify setting itself apart. The ego of the individual must take stronger and stronger measures in order to justify staying apart from the whole. These measures give rise to a series of dramas that are aimed at justifying the individual's separateness by actually causing other individuals to slow down their growth in awareness.

I am talking about a role – predefined or self-defined – in which you see yourself as part of the whole. I am talking about a drama in which you see yourself as apart from the whole. The role has no tension between you and others because no matter how you play it, it contributes to your own growth and to the growth of the whole—it adds to the momentum of the Holy Spirit in your unit. The drama has a built-in, inescapable tension between you and others.

In order to justify your position, you must seek to get others to validate your position. That means causing them to limit their own growth in self-awareness by getting them to likewise take on a drama instead of a role. When you are in a drama, there is constant conflict between yourself and other people. You are, in a sense, seeking to draw the rest of the universe into your drama and make it fit into the mental box defined by the drama.

Dramas and free will

A role is like the normal process of cell-division that leads one cell to grow into a complete human body. A drama is like a cancer that causes cells to self-destruct and then spreads to other cells until the whole body dies. This is the essential difference between roles and dramas. When you are playing a role, you do not feel threatened by anything and you can live and let live. When you are playing a drama, you constantly feel threatened. This inevitably leads you into seeking to control other people and your environment. This is also what makes you vulnerable to being pulled into the epic dramas, as we shall see in the next discourse.

In order to understand personal dramas, you need to fully understand free will, and this, of course, is the problem. Those who develop a drama do so precisely because they will not understand and accept how free will works. That is why – once they have stepped into a drama – they will think it was forced upon them and thus they must deny their ability to get out of it by their own power and choosing.

What is the essence of free will? Many people think that if they truly have free will, it means that they can do anything they want, with no restrictions. This view is perfectly correct. You do have free will and God has put no restrictions whatsoever on what you can do inside the energy environment in which you live. In the sandbox of the material universe, you can do anything you want, for nothing you do will hurt the sand.

However, while this view of free will is correct, it is not the complete understanding of free will. The world of form is a learning environment. How do you learn? By using your free will to express your co-creative abilities and then experiencing the result of your choice.

If your choice has no consequence – if there is no feed-back mechanism to signal the difference between choosing one option over a million other options – how can you learn and grow? If you make a choice and there is no feed-back, you have not actually made a choice.

What is the feed-back mechanism built into the world of form? It is that while you have free will, you will experience the consequences of your choices. One way of describing this is to say that the universe is a mirror. The Ma-ter light will outpicture physical circumstances that are a reflection of the beliefs, images and feelings you hold in your mind. You will project the images from your mental box upon the Ma-ter light that will take on the corresponding form.

While you do have free will, you also have full and complete responsibility for the choices you make! Why is this so important? Because when you accept full responsibility for yourself, you know that if a choice gives you unwanted feed-back, you can simply learn from it and make a better choice that will inevitably improve the feed-back! You are thus empowered and will never feel like a victim. You realize that with God within you, you have the power to change or transcend any circumstance.

The denial of free will

Once you accept a drama, you refuse to take responsibility. This means you no longer believe you have the power to change any circumstance. You believe you are a victim of forces beyond your control, but what is causing this? Only your refusal to take full responsibility for yourself!

This now leads to a further necessity, namely that those who will not take full responsibility for themselves, must rebel against or deny free will. If you do not take full responsibility for yourself, you do not believe you have truly free will, including the power to change any circumstance by changing your state of mind. This also means you do not fully respect the free will of others. You will fall prey to the serpentine lie that the ends can justify the means, which means you will seek to control others instead of taking dominion over your sphere of self. You will seek to control others in order to validate the ego's claim that you do not have to change by taking responsibility for yourself.

Furthermore, you do not respect your own free will, meaning you become open to following an external authority who will tell you what to believe and how to live. You become prone to being a blind follower of the blind leaders. You follow a false teacher rather than the true teacher that you turned your back upon when you refused to take responsibility for yourself. The blind leaders are, of course, those with epic dramas, as we will discuss in the coming discourse.

Why dramas seem real

The essence of a drama is that it is created in order to justify why a being does not take full responsibility for itself. It cannot be seen as merely a drama that is based on unreality and that you can walk away from—like a play in a theater. It must be defended, justified and validated as being based on absolute reality – as being the way life really is – and having a power over you that you cannot overcome by your own strength. You either need an external savior or you need to bring the drama to its ultimate conclusion by forcing others to enter your drama.

Any drama is created from duality, meaning it has two opposites that can only be in conflict. Conflict is built into the drama, which for the personal drama means conflict with other people or your physical environment. This means that people who live in a drama are constantly resisting the River of Life or the Holy Spirit. They are resisting the upward momentum of their entire sphere, which no individual and no group (at least not any minority group) has the power to do. This built-in resistance inevitably leads to suffering, which causes people to take themselves too seriously. Once you take yourself and your drama too seriously, it becomes a vicious circle that prevents you from returning to the River of Life through the playfulness of a little child. You simply cannot fathom or accept that you can just walk away from the drama. You think the drama must be brought to its self-defined conclusion and that the only way is to apply enough force to overcome the opposition to the drama's conclusion.

Because the opposition is created by the drama itself – your resistance to life – no amount of force available to you in the consciousness of the drama can overcome the opposition also created by the drama. Take the scientifically proven law of action and reaction. For every action there is an equal reaction, meaning it has the same force but the opposite direction. This law states that there is no decisive force, for no action can possibly be bigger than its self-generated reaction.

That is why I said that with men this is impossible, meaning that with the consciousness of a drama, it is not possible to generate a force that propels you out of the drama. Only by reaching for the power of God from within yourself can you generate a force that helps you transcend the drama. You can do this only when you let go of the drama, when you are willing to lose your "life" for my sake. Only then will there be a decisive force.

A personal drama will make you vulnerable to being pulled into an epic drama, and the epic drama is far greater than any individual. It is far more difficult for an individual to escape the maelstrom of the epic dramas. Obviously, it can be done, but only when you begin to see the fallacy, the vanity and the unreality of the epic dramas.

In my next discourse, I will explain the origin of the epic dramas so that you can become wise as the serpents and have the option to choose to be harmless as a dove. An option you do not have while trapped inside the mental box of an epic and a personal drama.

Mental boxes revisited

As my final thought, let me return to the concept of a mental box. When a new co-creator is created, it has a very localized perspective on the world and on itself. This perspective inevitably forms a mental box. When a new co-creator takes on a predefined role, the being's mental box will be affected by the role. As it transcends the role, it transcends the mental box of the role but may carry certain elements with it that it has incorporated into its personal mental box. This is not necessarily wrong, as the role is defined to facilitate the growth of the co-creator and thus contains timeless elements.

As long as a co-creator sees itself as part of a larger whole and is striving to expand its self-awareness, the mental box is not really a problem as it is constantly being expanded. As long as you constantly expand your mental box, any mental box can eventually be transcended so you reach the ascended state. A mental box simply gives the co-creator a foundation for functioning in the world while expanding its sense of self.

The problem comes in when a co-creator decides not to take full responsibility and creates a role as being apart from the whole. This role obviously necessitates the creation of another mental box, but this box is created by the ego and the ego is fully identified with it. To the ego, the defense of the mental box is a matter of life and death.

As long as a being has no drama, the being is not fully identified with its mental box. It has no need to hold on to an old mental box because it is constantly experiencing that expanding the box leads to a greater sense of self and a richer life. In this state, the Conscious You is not fully identified with the box and eventually comes to realize it is more than any mental box on earth. The box is a means to an end, not an end in itself. This is what I meant when I said that unless you become as a little child – eager to expand its mental box – you cannot enter the kingdom.

When a being creates a personal drama, the Conscious You retreats into a cave and now lets the ego take over its interactions with the world. You are no longer relating to the world as pure awareness but only through the filter of the drama, namely the ego and the spirits that spring from the drama. The ego is indeed fully identified with the mental box as it would have no life without it. The ego will defend your mental box to the death, even to the death of your physical body as proven by many people on earth.

The ego will even defend your mental box until you face the second death and there is only one way out. The Conscious You – *you* – must take back full responsibility for your life and stop identifying with the mental box created by the ego and the fallen beings. The catch-22 is that a mental box based on duality makes it difficult for you to even hear, let alone accept, this truth. The mental box of the ego has layers of built-in defenses designed to prevent you from taking back full responsibility for your life.

After spending many lifetimes in the ego's mental box, it can truly be very difficult for students to come to see the beam in their own eyes. It is so easy to accept the arguments presented by the ego and the false teachers. Just look at how many used their mental boxes to reject me 2,000 years ago. Nevertheless, we who are the true teachers of humankind are not deterred. We continue to release our core message in many different versions, knowing that for each time, some will understand.

In the coming discourses, I will indeed continue to expose the dramas so that you have the best possible opportunity for seeing how your own life is affected by this very subtle mechanism. May you be willing to lose the pseudo life of your mental box in order to follow me into the LIFE of the Christ consciousness where there are no dramas but only the purity of the innocent. May you be one of the meek who shall inherit the earth.

6 | THE ORIGIN OF EPIC
DRAMAS

We will now build on the foundation set in the previous discourse, and let us begin by taking another look at personal dramas. When a co-creator creates a personal drama, the drama is based on the co-creator's current perspective on the environment in which it lives, be that the material universe or a previous sphere. The co-creator is inside its sphere and is looking at life from that vantage point.

A co-creator cannot see its sphere from the outside, meaning it cannot fully understand how life, free will and the process of growth works. In order to fully understand how life works, the co-creator must first take full responsibility for itself, and if it did so, it would have no need to create a drama. By the very fact that the co-creator creates a drama, it is proven that it has not fully understood life. We might say that the co-creator looks at life from inside a particular mental box that presents a limited or even a distorted view.

What we now need to add is that co-creators are not the only beings created to assist in the ascension of a given sphere. Co-creators are the beings who are created to take on bodies made from the sphere's base energies and work on raising the sphere from the inside. There are also beings who are created to help a specific sphere by working from the outside, from the higher level(s) of the sphere. These beings are what people on earth normally call angels.

When a co-creator wins its ascension, it becomes an ascended master. Many religious people believe angels are created as permanent beings, but that raises the question of how angels could fall. The explanation is that there are ascended angels and unascended angels. For each new sphere, many angels are created to serve that sphere and they do not become permanent beings until their sphere ascends and they ascend.

Although angels are not meant to take embodiment, they still have free will, for how else could they grow in self-awareness? When an angel is created to serve a particular sphere, it also has a limited self-awareness. Because it is not in a body, it has a wider perspective on its sphere than the co-creators who are looking at it from the inside. This means that as a sphere rises in vibration, the angel has the opportunity to gain a broader understanding of how God's creation works, including free will. A co-creator can also gain this understanding but only after it has taken full responsibility for itself and has no need to create the dramas that will prevent a co-creator from seeing the full truth.

The test of angels

Here comes the all-important distinction. The growth of a sphere is dependent upon one thing and one thing only, namely the growth in self-awareness of the co-creators who embody in the sphere. The angels who serve a sphere can contribute to the growth of the sphere, but they can do so only by assisting the co-creators who are inside the sphere. This assistance can be given only within the context of free will. An angel has no right – and indeed has no direct power – to force or overrule the free will of co-creators.

When a group of co-creators refuse to take responsibility for themselves and start creating personal dramas, the angels can clearly see how this will limit the co-creators and the growth of their sphere. If the co-creators refuse the assistance offered by the angels, the angels can do nothing but simply watch as the co-creators generate a downward spiral. If a majority of the co-creators in a sphere refused to grow, the angels could only stand by (if their help was rejected) and watch as the entire sphere disintegrated. Likewise, if a group of co-creators refuse to transcend their dramas when their sphere ascends, the angels can only watch as they fall into the next sphere and are lost to their original sphere.

What is the test of angels? A co-creator comes to a point where it has to take full and final responsibility for itself. Instead, the angel faces the challenge of allowing the process of free will to outplay itself freely—meaning that the angel must allow co-creators to express their free will in any way they want. In order to pass this test, the angel must acquire a complete understanding of free will, and it must come to respect free will with the same absolute acceptance that the Creator has. In passing, let me mention that ascended masters have acquired this understanding and acceptance by taking embodiment and ascending, a perspective that angels naturally do not have. This explains why ascended masters have no problem with the test that can be difficult for many unascended angels.

Another way to say this is that a co-creator faces the test of fully accepting its own free will whereas an angel faces the test of fully accepting the free will of others. If you look more closely, it is actually the same test from different vantage points. When you take full responsibility for yourself, you come to have full respect for your own free will, and this also gives you full respect for the free will of others.

If an angel does not develop full respect for the free will of others, it is because the angel has not taken full responsibility for itself (if the angel did, it would know that it can grow in self-awareness even if co-creators do not). When you do take full responsibility for yourself, you also accept that you are not responsible for the choices made by other self-aware beings. When an angel fails the test of free will, it actually develops an inappropriate sense of responsibility for the co-creators it was meant to serve. As we shall see, this false responsibility gives rise to the desire to force co-creators.

What happens when an angel faces this test and refuses to rise to a higher understanding and acceptance of the Law of Free Will? The angel is actually faced with a test that is as important as that faced by co-creators when their teachers require them to take full responsibility and define their own roles. The angel is likewise guided by a leader, and if the angel will not accept free will, then the angel must do what co-creators do in order to justify their rejection of the teacher and the lesson.

Rebellion of angels

When an angel fails the test of unconditional acceptance of the free will of co-creators, the angel can do this only by creating a drama. This drama is somewhat similar to the dramas created by co-creators, only it is based on the viewpoint – the mental box – of the angels. It is based on a greater perspective and understanding of how life works than the inside perspective of co-creators. This gives rise to a different possibility. The personal dramas created by co-creators are based on the duality consciousness and they have a built-in tension that causes a co-creator to rebel against authority in its own sphere – its spiritual teacher – and to generate conflict with other co-creators. The angel, however, does have some overall understanding of how life works, and this means it can rebel against the entire process of growth in self-awareness. A co-creator can only rebel against what it sees, namely its spiritual teachers and other co-creators. An angel can rebel against God and the Creator's purpose and design, specifically the decision to give co-creators free will.

This means that the dramas created by co-creators are directed outward (horizontally) in their own sphere whereas the dramas created by angels are directed upward and downward (vertically). The angels come to believe that the Creator was wrong for giving co-creators free will so they want to prove God and free will wrong.

They also believe they are responsible for the growth of co-creators and that co-creators should be forced to do what is in their own best interest—according to the definition of the angels. In a sense we might say that all dramas are control games. Co-creators want to control their spiritual teachers and other co-creators. Angels want to control God and all co-creators.

This explains why I have made the distinction between the personal dramas of co-creators and the epic dramas created by angels. The angels can create dramas that take the duality consciousness to its ultimate extreme by portraying God as one dualistic polarity that is opposed by another dualistic polarity of equal strength—or at least of such strength that there is a real battle and a real potential for God to lose some souls. Co-creators simply could not create such a drama from their limited perspective. Only the unascended angels have the perspective – without the full understanding – to create such an epic drama.

How angels fell

As explained in the previous discourse, there came a point in the fourth sphere when a number of co-creators started creating personal dramas. At that point, certain bands of angels were assigned to assist these co-creators and use legitimate means to help them transcend their dramas—means that do not violate the free will of the co-creators. As the sphere was ready to ascend, it became obvious that a number of co-creators (a large number compared to the population of the earth but a very small number compared to the total number of co-creators in the sphere) were not willing to leave behind their personal dramas. They would not be able to ascend with their sphere, and preparations were made for having them descend to the next sphere that was being created.

What happened next was that a portion of the angels assigned to assist these co-creators began to feel that this was wrong and that the co-creators were being lost. Over time of working with the co-creators, these angels had developed a certain sense of superiority because the angels could easily see the shortcomings of the dramas created by the co-creators. The angels could see that the co-creators would only hurt themselves, and they could easily see through the arguments that the co-creators used to defend their dramas—even as they argued with the spiritual teachers sent to assist them. These angels developed a sense of superiority compared to those they considered less sophisticated than themselves, those whom they saw as below them.

At the same time, the angels also began to feel that the impending loss of these co-creators proved that the Creator's plan was flawed. They began to feel that they could have easily forced the co-creators to ascend, and thus they began to feel that they knew better than the Creator how life should work.

This became a spiritual pride, and combined with a false sense of responsibility (the angels felt they should have been able to force co-creators to make right choices), it became a "fog" of confusion that the angels could not see through.

The pride of the angels made them feel that they should not admit that they had failed their assigned task. In truth, no one had asked them to admit that they had failed for no one who understood free will thought that the angels had failed— as the angels had no way to force co-creators. The problem was that the angels failed the test of taking full responsibility for themselves. If they had done so, they would have known that they were not responsible for the choices made by co-creators. They could have set the co-creators free to have any experience they wanted, and they could have "set God free" to design the universe the only way it can lead to ultimate self-awareness.

All in all, this led the angels – and especially a few of their leaders who felt the greatest sense of responsibility – to develop a set of dramas that I have called epic dramas. The reason is that while these dramas were developed by the angels much as the personal dramas of co-creators, they are based on the view that there is a flaw or injustice in the universe that the angels (or whomever plays these dramas) are meant to correct. Epic dramas have a much wider scope than personal dramas.

The consequence is that these angels fell into the next sphere with their epic dramas, and they immediately began to seek to draw new co-creators into them. This became possible only when co-creators started creating their own personal dramas, which then made them open to the epic dramas. The epic dramas seemed to offer the perfect justification sought through the personal dramas. Of course, you also had the co-creators who had descended from the fourth sphere and they were open to the epic dramas right away.

As a side note, take note that an angel was not created to take embodiment. When an angel falls, it does not descend into the next sphere as an angel but as a being that takes embodiment. It therefore becomes like a co-creator that operates within a denser body than the angels created to assist the new sphere. These newly created angels have not fallen.

The fifth sphere saw co-creators who developed a drama that was a mixture of the personal dramas and the epic dramas. Some of these co-creators could not ascend with the fifth sphere and have continued to fall into the present sphere, the seventh. You now have a number of lifestreams – from a background of both angels and co-creators – who came into this sphere with a well-developed set of personal and epic dramas.

Obviously, when a being has not developed its drama in the present sphere, a new level of difficulty comes into play. It is almost inevitable that such a being feels superior to the new co-creators in the present sphere. This spiritual pride makes it much more difficult to develop the humbleness of a little child and the willingness to listen to a spiritual teacher. Instead, these beings tend to not only reject but to actively oppose spiritual teachers. It was indeed such beings who opposed me and eventually had me crucified. A spiritual teacher will allow himself to be exposed to this in order to give such beings a last opportunity to see their dramas.

7 | THE ESSENTIAL FLAW OF DRAMAS

Let us look at the essence of a drama. A personal drama makes it seem like your salvation is dependent upon you achieving something in your sphere, something that cannot be completed without the co-operation of other people. The epic drama makes it seem like the salvation of the world cannot be completed without achieving something in this world, such as making Christianity the only religion on earth.

The central illusion is that the drama is not a drama but reality. You will believe that either yourself or the world will not be saved until the goal defined by the drama has been achieved physically. Because this goal is defined based on an illusion, it can never be achieved, meaning that you are pursuing an impossible goal. You can seek this goal indefinitely, and the only way out of this impossible quest is to come to see the unreality of the drama.

Why is it easier to escape a personal drama than an epic drama? A personal drama is a struggle between you and some authority figure and other people within your own sphere. You are trying to prove yourself right and the others wrong, but you are not trying to prove that God is wrong or that the entire universe is based on a flawed design. A personal drama is clearly centered around you, and there is at least some possibility that you will eventually come to realize that the only way to change your outer situation is to change yourself.

When it comes to the epic drama, you have not only refused to take responsibility for yourself, you have projected that responsibility upon a force that is on a much bigger scale, such as God, the universe or humankind at large. It now becomes possible to believe that the cause for which your drama makes it seem like you are fighting is so big that it could not possibly be resolved by you or could not be resolved in one lifetime. This gives you an even more watertight excuse for not looking at yourself but continuing to project responsibility outside yourself, projecting it on forces or circumstances that a human being on earth could not possible influence alone.

We might say that the personal drama revolves around "me, myself and I," which keeps it on a scale that at least has the focus on you. When you begin to see through the drama, you can relatively easily see that you do indeed have the power to overcome the drama by changing yourself. The epic drama projects responsibility so far away that it makes it more difficult for lifestreams to accept that they still have the power to overcome the drama. It is easier to see that a personal drama is created in the mind whereas it is far more difficult to see that this is also the case for the epic dramas.

What makes a lifestream susceptible to the epic dramas? It is the lifestream's personal dramas because the epic dramas tie in to the personal dramas and offer an even more watertight excuse for not looking at the beam in your own eye. If you believe there really is a Battle of Armageddon between God and the devil, and if you believe other people are on the side of the devil, then you can easily believe that you have no reason to look at the beam in your own eye—for you are obviously on the good side. You simply have to keep fighting the bad side until the battle is won—which might happen any day or in a thousand years, but in either case postponing the decision to look in the mirror.

The essence of a drama is that you think the fulfillment of your goals in life (even your salvation) depends on the choices made by other people. The drama makes it seem like you are not responsible for your own destiny. The people around you are, and you have to try to force their will. Epic dramas add that in order to ensure the fulfillment of God's plan, in order for people to be saved, in order for the battle of Armageddon to be won, you must deal with the free will of all human beings. Instead of just saving yourself, you now have to save the entire universe.

The net effect of this illusion is that it focuses attention on the splinters in the eyes of other people. This causes people who have taken on the drama to use the drama's "perfect" excuse for not looking at the beam in their own eyes. Why is this a problem? Here is another absolute statement: As long as you are not looking at the beam in your own eye, you are not growing! It really is that simple and there is no way around it.

This is precisely what the dramas make it difficult for people to see. In the previous discourse I said that once you enter a drama, you can no longer see it as a drama. You think that the view of life – the mental box – presented by the drama is real, that it represents the way life really works. You now have the "perfect" excuse for not even considering that the drama is unreal, that it has no more reality than what you – and other people – give to it. You refuse to see that you can indeed walk away from the drama any time.

Consider what you would say about an actor who had become convinced that he really was Hamlet and who refused to take off the costume, insisting on playing the role even out-side the theater and claiming he really was the prince of Den-mark. You would probably think the person had lost touch with reality. Yet your own personal drama has the exact same effect—it causes you to lose touch with reality. What is the exact effect of this?

Why dramas make you unteachable

Let me first restate an absolute and inescapable fact. The Law of Free Will is the fundamental law of the world of form. You can become a permanent being – an ascended being – only by freely choosing to enter into oneness—oneness with your source and oneness with all life, with the whole. In order to make this choice, you must free your mind from all influence from the consciousness of separation, the consciousness of duality, the consciousness of anti-christ. All dramas are created out of this consciousness so it follows that you cannot make your ascension until you give up any and all dramas.

A drama forms a mental box and the box is closed. Any drama is based on an illusion, a view of reality that is out of touch with reality. This does not mean that the view is com-pletely false. It may indeed contain many ideas that are true in themselves, but the way they are presented in context means that the entire world view cannot lead you to the ascension.

The problem is that once you step inside the mental box defined by the drama, you can no longer see that the world view is an illusion. Instead, from your vantage point inside the box, you think the world view is real, that the world really is the way it appears from inside the mental box of the drama. It is like my often-used example that if you put on yellow glasses, you think the sky really is green.

What is the logical conclusion? When you are inside the mental box of a particular drama, you believe in an illusion. You also believe that this illusion is reality, and this is what makes it a catch-22 that is very difficult to escape.

Consider how the situation looks from the vantage point of a spiritual teacher. The teacher knows your world view is based on an illusion. He knows that the only way you can ascend is to help you see through the illusion. What is the most natural way to seek to help you? It would be a two-fold approach of seeking to present you with a correct world view while pointing out the flaws in your existing world view.

Now consider how you will experience the teacher's attempts to help you when you see them from inside the box. You think your view is reality, and thus what this self-appointed spiritual teacher is presenting to you can only be unreality. He must be a false teacher and anything he says must be meant to deceive you and make you believe a lie instead of the reality you already have.

The subtle mechanism that comes into play here is that if the Conscious You identifies itself fully with the drama, your mind will be closed to anything that a spiritual teacher could possibly say to you. Nothing could penetrate the defenses erected by your mental box. Anything that goes beyond or contradicts your existing world view will be rejected. In order to help you escape your limited world view, the teacher must of necessity give you knowledge that contradicts or goes beyond your existing world view.

How come some people actually manage to listen to spiritual teachers? Because after having outplayed their dramas for a sufficient amount of time, their conscious selves have begun to doubt the world view presented by its drama. The Conscious You has begun to separate itself from the drama so that it can start opening itself to an outside perspective on the drama—what is presented by the spiritual teacher.

Projections versus understanding

As I have said, the entire world of form is designed to facilitate the growth in self-awareness. The Creator is not unintelligent and foresaw what could happen as a result of free will. There are a number of built-in safeguards that are designed to ensure that while self-aware beings can indeed enter into a mental box, these mental boxes will inevitably be challenged. Once you step into a drama, the world view presented by the drama will be seen as being under constant attack. Consequently, those affected by the drama are constantly having to defend their view as the only real view of life, as the highest and absolute truth, as the only true religion or belief system.

When you feel that your world view is indeed the way life is – and you experience that it is under threat from unreality – your only way to defend your "truth" is to go into a state of mind that is based on projecting. You are constantly projecting your mental image upon yourself, God, the world and other people. You are seeking to force the universe to fit into your mental box by projecting the box and a very aggressive intent upon others.

Obviously, this is a violation of the free will of others, but you don't see it that way. You think that others are opposing the only truth, the one defined by your mental box. They are violating your free will and you have a right – indeed a sacred duty – to defend truth. The problem is that when you go into this mindset, your mind becomes closed to a spiritual teacher. The reason is that your mind is fully focused on – filled with – the need to project your existing mental image upon everything. There is no awareness of the need to expand your world view. Your mind is a one-way street with plenty of output but no room for input. You think you already have the highest truth so what is the need for you to open your mind to a higher understanding?

How will you ever escape your current drama? Only by becoming open to a broader world view than what you see from inside the mental box defined by the drama. How could you possibly see such a broader world view? Only when your mind stops projecting and becomes at least somewhat open to input from a higher source. You must stop projecting and seek to understand. We can also say that the Conscious You must stop projecting itself through the drama and project itself outside the drama in order to experience pure awareness or the input from a spiritual teacher or its I AM Presence. As I have said before, you can never lose this ability but you can indeed forget it and that is the most limiting effect of dramas.

A drama – and especially the state of mind in which you are projecting – makes you unteachable. You are simply unreachable for a spiritual teacher, who must respect your free will and withdraw until the built-in safety mechanisms have – through the School of Hard Knocks – worn down your assuredness in your drama's reality to the point where you are again open to understanding.

Observe your own reaction

I will go into more detail in coming discourses, but for now let me leave you to ponder one thought. The effect of the drama is that you resist the River of Life and you resist the teacher's instructions. If you are honest with yourself, you can use your reactions to these discourses to gain some perspective on your personal drama. Do you find a certain resistance in yourself to my words? If so, follow the feelings and thoughts to their source and you might indeed discover why you are resisting. Do you find that you are projecting an existing view onto my teachings and using it to judge, analyze or evaluate everything I say? Do you find that there is a process – almost subconscious – aimed at invalidating my teachings so that you have a justification for not truly seeking to understand your own drama? Are you truly open to understanding what I am saying or are you seeking to reject it so that you do not have to look at the beam in your own eye?

There are many people who have used their existing mental box to judge a spiritual teaching as being false or impure as an excuse for not heeding the teaching. These people overlook a very simple fact. There is no spiritual teaching that will automatically awaken everybody. If it was possible to formulate a teaching that was guaranteed to awaken any person who studied it, humankind would already have ascended. The effect of a teaching is not dependent upon the teaching. It is dependent exclusively on what the person studying it is willing to do with the teaching. Does the person have an open mind, is he or she seeking to understand rather than to project?

As I explain throughout my website, official Christianity has grossly distorted my original teachings. Over the past 2,000 years a few people have still been able to use these distorted teachings to qualify for their ascensions. I admit there have not been many, but even a distorted or partially false teaching contains enough truth that a student who is willing to transcend the outer teaching can still make progress.

Your progress does not depend on anything outside yourself. It depends exclusively on your willingness to take responsibility for yourself. It depends only on the choices you make. The basic choice for any spiritual student is this: Do you want to project and reject, or do you want to understand and expand? It is your drama that causes you to reject a higher understanding. If you reject the understanding I have hidden between the lines of these discourses, it is your drama that causes your rejection. There can be no other explanation, even if your drama offers you one.

Your drama is designed to project responsibility away from you, and thus it will seek to place responsibility anywhere else. As long as you are projecting responsibility outside yourself, you cannot do the one thing that can help you escape your drama, namely to take full responsibility for yourself. You cannot overcome your drama until you accept that you have created or accepted it and that you are the only one who can change that choice.

The choice is whether you will look at yourself and seek to unmask the drama or whether you will continue to project that the drama is right and that I am wrong. If you reject the understanding I offer you, you must continue to affirm the drama—indefinitely.

I am in full acceptance of your right to choose, and I am in full acceptance of *you* regardless of what you choose. I also accept the fact that those who continue to project and reject have set themselves outside of my Circle of Oneness and they are unteachable to me. I am here to help those who are willing to transcend their dramas. I am not here to validate anyone's drama, and I proved that by letting myself be killed as the ultimate way to expose people's dramas. How far does the Living Christ have to go with you before your drama becomes so extreme that you are willing to look at it?

A foundational truth

When you are playing a role instead of a drama, there is no conflict between you and life and you have no need to resist the flow of the River of Life. You even have no need to resist the dramas outplayed by other people, for you do not allow yourself to take in the consciousness of the dramas.

This leaves us with only one plausible conclusion. Any time you resist anything – whether you resist life or whether you resist the dramas of other people, even resist the devil himself – your resistance is exclusively a product of your personal drama combined with any epic drama you have accepted. There simply is no other explanation, for only a drama makes it seem necessary to resist anything—including the dramas of other people.

Once some beings have developed dramas, it becomes a subtle temptation for other beings to develop their own dramas in order to resist the dramas that the first people are seeking to force upon them. That is precisely how dramas spread like a cancer until a downward spiral forms that only very few individuals have the non-attachment to transcend.

If you have no drama, you are non-attached to any circumstance you encounter, and you do not use it as an excuse for not letting your light shine. When you are focused on letting your light shine, you have no attention left over for resisting—you are untouched by the dramas of others. You are simply being the Sun of God who is radiating your light independently of other people or material circumstances. This is the only way to secure your own ascension and make your personal contribution to the ascension of the world, meaning the ascension of your sphere.

May the prince of this world come and find no drama in you whereby he can tempt you to react to and resist anything in this world.

8 | WHY PEOPLE CLING TO THEIR DRAMAS

One of the most subtle and difficult to recognize effects of a drama is that it creates a mental box. As a result, people in the box are constantly projecting mental images upon everything that happens to them. Even a teaching that talks about dramas will be read by people through their personal filters, meaning they will superimpose their mental images upon the teaching and – depending on their particular drama – find cause to either reject the teaching outright or (the most common reaction) see how it applies to other people while failing to see how it applies to themselves.

The one fundamental realization that is the foundation for all spiritual progress is that: "There is something I don't know." There is something you do not see, there is a veil that prevents you from seeing a reality that is beyond your own mental box and the collective mental box of humankind. The Buddha called it the "veil of Maya," and I talked about it in various ways, including the beam in your own eye and calling for those who have eyes to see and ears to hear. In this day and age, we can be a lot more specific.

Quantum physics and mental boxes

The findings of quantum physics are revolutionary in many ways. In this context, let us begin with the fact that quantum physics has proven that for a human being it is impossible to make a truly objective observation, meaning an observation that is not affected by your mind. In classical physics, the universe was divided into two realms, a realm of matter that existed independently of any mind (and was objective) and the realm of mind that was entirely subjective. By using proper instruments and procedures, scientists could – so it was claimed – make an observation that was not affected by their minds.

What quantum physics has shown is that the realm of matter is an illusion created by the physical senses and a particular mindset, a particular mental box. The deeper truth is that consciousness is the fundamental reality and that matter is a creation of consciousness. Quantum physics talks about this by saying that everything that exists is made from quantum waveforms, which in reality are mental images superimposed upon the Ma-ter light by self-aware beings.

What is currently keeping quantum physicists in a deadlock is that they will not acknowledge that there are self-aware beings who are not human beings and that these beings have also superimposed mental images upon the Ma-ter light. Scientists are left to ponder such questions as: "Is the moon really there if no one is looking?" The reality is that the moon truly is there even when no *human* being is looking because the moon was created by spiritual beings who are always looking.

There is something which we might call an objective reality, in the sense that it was not created by human beings, meaning beings trapped in the duality consciousness. The earth in its pure form was created by the Elohim and the spiritual realm was (and is) created by higher beings. There is indeed a reality that is not affected by the duality consciousness and its illusions.

You will not be able to perceive this reality in its fullest as long as you are looking at life through any mental box. The reason being that as long as you are looking through a mental box, you will inevitably project the mental images from the box upon everything you see. As quantum physics explains it, the act of observation is influenced by your consciousness. What you see is a product of an interaction between the quantum waveform of your consciousness and the quantum waveform of whatever you are observing.

The conclusion is that as long as you are looking though a mental box, you cannot see the reality created by spiritual beings (at least not fully). Instead, you are seeing something that *you* have created by superimposing your own mental images (or the collective images of your "group") upon that objective reality.

As an example, consider a fundamentalist Christian who finds my website. He or she is looking through a particular mental box and is very attached to having that mental box confirmed. As soon as the person finds something on the site that does not confirm the mental box, the only possible reaction is to reject the site. Did the person actually hear what I am saying, or did the person only "hear" an echo created by his or her consciousness superimposing a fixed mental image upon my words? Now take this one step further and be willing to look in the mirror. No matter who you are, no matter how long you have been on the spiritual path, no matter how many teachings you have studied or what techniques you have practiced, you are also looking at my words through your current mental box. The essential dividing line between those who are teachable for a spiritual teacher and those who are not is the following realization:

• I too have a mental box.

• It does inevitably affect the way I look at everything, including the spiritual teacher/teaching.

• I do not see how my mental box is affecting my vision of everything and the conclusions I draw based on my observations. I tend to think that what my mental box is showing me is reality.

• I need a spiritual teacher precisely because I cannot, on my own, see beyond my mental box.

• My ability to make progress depends on my willingness to let the teacher challenge my mental box and show me its inconsistencies and limitations.

• I only make progress to the extent that I allow the teacher to show me what I cannot see.

• If I seek to protect and defend my mental box, I close my mind to the teacher's help and become unteachable.

• It is my responsibility to keep my mind and heart open to the teacher by being willing to question everything. It is my responsibility to continually purify my mind of all dualistic illusions, even the most subtle ones that seem like absolute truth. What I am not willing to question becomes my prison.

One might say that the central question is whether you want to defend your current mental box/drama by projecting and rejecting or whether you will let the teacher open your mind to a higher vision of reality by seeking to understand and expand. Most people on earth are completely unaware of the fact that what they see is not reality but a product of their own mental images superimposed upon not only reality but the distorted "reality" created by humankind for eons.

I have said that you will have a mental box as long as you are in embodiment. However, as you do purify your mind, the Conscious You can begin to disassociate itself from your mental box. Because the Conscious You is an extension of the Creator's Being, it can step outside of any mental box and experience an objective reality. Having such an experience is extremely valuable. However, as Maitreya explains in greater detail in his book, once you come back to your normal awareness, you will inevitably look at and interpret the experience through your mental box. We again see the need to continually purify your mind of dualistic illusions so that you do not seek to force a transcendent, infinite experience to fit into a finite mental box.

Growth is a product of your life experience

Let us again look at classical physics and the claim of an objective reality. In a sense, this claim is not wrong, merely incomplete. As I have explained, there is a reality that was not created by the minds of human beings in duality and one could call this an objective reality. The problem with classical physics was that it portrayed this reality as a mechanical "device" that functions according to invariable and deterministic laws, meaning that the fate of the universe was determined from the beginning. Human beings can only observe but cannot influence the clockwork universe. Quantum physics has proven this to be incorrect because there is a fundamental uncertainty in the universe. Events are not predetermined, but a particular outcome is selected only as an observation is made—and the consciousness of the observer is co-creating the outcome.

Now let us look at the situation of a new co-creator that comes into existence. The co-creator is aware that it exists in an environment that it has not created (environmental awareness) and it is aware that it exists as an individual being in that environment (self-awareness). Compare this to a baby on earth. The baby has an awareness of its immediate environment, such as its nursery, but it has no awareness of anything beyond what it can observe. Some babies have self-awareness while others have very little. As the baby grows, there is an expansion of its environmental awareness and self-awareness.

The baby gradually becomes aware that the room it can see is only one room in a larger unit, namely a house. It then becomes aware of itself as a being within that house. Next, it becomes aware that the house is in a larger unit, called a garden. It then becomes aware that there are other houses in a neighborhood. Then it realizes there are many neighborhoods in its city, that there are other cities in its country, other countries in the world and so on. As the child grows into an adult, it might travel all over the world and expand both its environmental awareness and its self-awareness (as part of a larger whole) far beyond what it was as a baby.

Likewise, a new co-creator starts out with a highly localized environmental awareness and self-awareness and it gradually expands both. As part of the expansion of environmental awareness, the co-creator becomes aware that there is indeed a larger reality with which it can interact. This starts with awareness of its immediate environment but ideally expands until the co-creator sees the material universe as a whole and also sees the spiritual world beyond it. This larger reality was not created by itself, but it does respond to the co-creator's actions and choices.

As part of the expansion of self-awareness, the co-creator will ideally become aware that although there is an external reality, the co-creator's experience of that reality, of life and of itself is not taking place "out there" but "in here." The normal growth in self-awareness makes a co-creator aware that its purpose for existence is to grow in self-awareness and that this growth happens as a result of what is going on inside its own mind, namely its life experience. We could say that environmental awareness can be forced upon you from without whereas the growth in self-awareness can happen only from within, as a result of your life experience.

When a co-creator becomes aware of this, it realizes that its external environment is reacting to its internal environment. As I have said many times, the universe is a mirror. When you begin to see this, you realize that your state of mind has a major impact on both your external circumstances and how you react to or experience those circumstances—and this is when you begin to grow consciously.

If we use the language of quantum physics, you begin to realize that your environment is a quantum waveform and so is your consciousness. Your life experience is a product of the interaction between the two waveforms. In the beginning, it will seem like your mind does not have the power to directly change your environment, but as a co-creator grows, it begins to realize that it has the power to change the contents of its mind, and this will have a direct impact on its life experience.

Taking command over your life experience

To put it simply, if you take a positive attitude to life, your life experience will improve whereas a negative attitude will cause your life experience to deteriorate. Regardless of your outer circumstances, there is always something you can do to improve your life experience, namely to change the contents of your mind, your container of self. As you adopt a more positive attitude, you realize that you are now attracting (actually co-creating, although this awareness usually comes later) more positive outer circumstances.

This stage of conscious growth leads toward the point I described in the previous discourses where your teacher will confront you with the need to become spiritually self-sufficient by accepting full responsibility for your ability to take dominion over your life experience. Instead of playing predefined roles, you now define your own role, define what kind of experience you want to have in the material universe. The entire universe is designed to facilitate your own growth in self-awareness, which means that you have both the capacity and the right to create your own life experience. The external reality created by higher beings has only one purpose, namely to allow you to create any experience you desire, and the Ma-ter light will literally take on any mental image projected upon it.

Some co-creators take this initiation with enthusiasm and immediately start experimenting while others are reluctant. It is much like a writer who is facing a blank sheet of paper upon which anything can be written. Suddenly, the person has writer's block and cannot write anything at all. The same can happen to a painter who faces a blank canvas—he or she is overwhelmed by the total freedom to create absolutely anything.

Why does this happen? Up until this point the co-creator has looked upon the external reality as something it could not change. Its life experience has been seen as a product of interacting with and adapting to the external reality created by others. Now it needs to realize the – for some shocking – truth that it has the capacity to create any experience for itself that it desires. It can redefine its external environment, but it can also use any existing environment to grow by changing its inner experience of the environment. Up until now the co-creator has believed that its life experience was shaped at least partly by external factors. It now needs to take full responsibility by accepting that there is nothing outside itself that can influence its life experience.

Some co-creators have come to feel secure in an environment that is defined by others, and they feel they have to give up this security in order to define their own life experience. Some want to keep reacting to circumstances created by others, and they are reluctant to admit that they can create their own circumstances. Some are content in the belief that their life experience is dependent upon outer circumstances and are reluctant to admit that it is completely created by themselves. It is comparable to college students who would rather stay in school than graduate and get a job.

The central question here is whether the co-creator will take full responsibility for itself and accept that it can define any experience it desires to have and that the external environment is not a limitation. If a co-creator accepts full responsibility, it will define a role that enhances both its own growth, the growth of other co-creators and the growth of the universe. If the co-creator does not take full responsibility, it has to justify this (in its own mind) by creating a drama. The reason is that when you do not take full responsibility, you will not accept the basic fact that you create your own life experience. You must create a drama that is based on the following illusions:

• You live in a world where there is an external reality that you did not create and that will not respond to your mind's abilities. You have only limited options for changing your environment.

- Your inner environment – your life experience – is wholly or partly determined by your external environment. You have only limited options for taking command over your mind and creating your own life experience. Only if external conditions change, will your internal conditions change.

- You do not have complete freedom to create any experience you want, for you are being forced by something outside yourself, be it God, the devil, a spiritual teacher, other people or the Great Pumpkin Man. You have to resist this external force in order to get what you want.

Instead of admitting that you are an extension of God and that with God all things are possible, you come to believe that you cannot change the external environment. You begin to see it as something that imposes restrictions upon you. This leads to a world view similar to that espoused by classical physics and even contemporary materialism, namely that there is an objective universe with natural laws that you can do nothing about. The psychological effect is that you now have the perfect excuse for not taking responsibility for yourself and for not creating your own life experience.

You no longer see yourself as a co-creator with unlimited potential, but you see yourself as a being who is forced by an external God to live in and adapt to an external environment. Because you do not have the power to change your external environment, you have no power to determine your life experience, as it will inevitably be determined by the environment, external events and other people. Instead of accepting that you have total freedom to create any life experience you desire to have, you see your life experience as a product of factors over which you have no control.

Denying your potential

The purpose of the universe is the growth of self-awareness of individual lifestreams. This growth is a product of your life experience. Taking full responsibility for yourself means accepting that regardless of your environment and the actions of other beings, you are creating your own inner experience. If you desire to go beyond your current or previous experiences, there is some place in this vast universe where you can either fit into an existing environment or create your own environment in order to have that experience. Regardless of your external environment, you are still able to have any inner experience you want.

We might say that when you accept full responsibility for yourself, you become self-determined in that you determine your life experience. When you deny responsibility, you become other-determined, in that you create or accept a drama that defines your life experience as being the product of external causes. Even then, your life experience is still the key to your growth and to your escape from the drama.

Let me say this in a different way. When you are trapped in a drama, you think your life experience (what happens inside of you) is wholly or partly dependent upon what happens outside of you, your external circumstances. Your only way to change your life experience is to change something outside of you. This is what keeps you trapped in a drama that promises you that when certain outer conditions are met, then will you be happy, at peace or whatever it may be. When you truly understand the path, you see that it is *your* responsibility to take command over your life experience and create the life experience you want independently of external circumstances. When you do take command over your internal circumstances, you realize that your external circumstances will begin to mirror the internal. The reason being that the universe is a mirror that can only reflect back what you project through your mind.

Your life experience determines your external circumstances, not the other way around. It is only when you change the internal that the external begins to change. That is why a drama will indefinitely prevent you from achieving your goals—because it keeps you trapped in the illusion that you have to change the external first, that you have to keep putting the cart before the horse

Who are you?

What is a drama? It is an illusion that defines you as a being who is less than what you really are. You are a spiritual being with the potential to take command over matter. It is not mind over matter but Spirit over matter. The drama makes you believe that you either are not a spiritual being or that even though you are a spiritual being, matter has power over you and can thus define your life experience.

How do you escape a drama? There is only one way. You must come to see through the illusions defined by the drama so you no longer accept that the material world can limit your Spirit. We of the ascended masters have proven this and that is why we are ascended. The question we will consider next is what options we have for helping unascended beings prove this so they can also accept it as reality. How can we help people transcend their dramas?

In order to fully understand this, we have to take a closer look at a very subtle effect of dramas. In order to explain this effect, we first have to take a closer look at who you are. As I explain this, keep in mind that your existing world view and understanding will form a mental box that will impact your ability to truly understand the (admittedly limited) words through which I have to communicate.

I have talked about the situation of a new co-creator, but what exactly is a new co-creator, how does such a being function, how does it look at itself and the world, what is going on in its mind? A new co-creator is a self-aware being, but what exactly does this mean? One way – and certainly not the only way – to describe this is to say that self-awareness has two aspects, namely pure awareness and the contents of awareness, the awareness of something. There is "awareness" and there is "self."

Most people will immediately wonder what pure awareness is, and the reason is that they have not experienced it in conscious memory. The reason is that they have come to identify themselves so completely with their current mental box that they cannot still the mind. They cannot look beyond the awareness of some object and experience pure awareness. One of the major benefits of meditative practices is the experience of this pure awareness. It inevitably changes your self-image because you realize that you have a self that is more than the contents of the container of self. Your awareness is more than your current self.

Looking at a new co-creator

If you took a new co-creator and put it in an environment with no forms and no external stimuli, the co-creator would still have pure awareness. It would be aware that it exists, and it would be aware that it is an extension of something beyond itself. However, the co-creator would remain in this awareness indefinitely, meaning that it would not grow as it has nothing to relate to, no way to express itself. That is why a new co-creator is placed in a predefined environment and given a role to play. This gives the co-creator something to relate to and a way to express itself. As it adapts to the external environment and expresses itself, it begins to develop a sense of self, a sense of who it is in relation to its environment.

We now have two components of self, namely the original pure awareness and the sense of self developed in response to a particular environment. The original pure awareness is what we have called the Conscious You because it is awareness that is beyond anything in the world of form. It is your ability – safety mechanism – that allows you to always know that you are more than any self you have defined in the world of form. I am quite aware that unless you have had a direct experience of this pure awareness, the concept of the Conscious You will be just that: a concept upon which you will project the mental images from your current mental box.

The explanation for this is that a new co-creator usually becomes so absorbed in playing its predefined role that it forgets its pure awareness and its connection to its source. It quickly creates a sense of self in relation to its environment, and it easily forgets that it is more than that sense of self. This is comparable to a baby, who often has an awareness of past lives but forgets this as it becomes involved with its present life. As we have said, the Conscious You truly is who it is, but in the here and now, the Conscious You is – for all practical purposes – who it thinks it is, who it sees itself as being.

This forgetting of your source is not a sin and is not the fall into duality. It is simply an inevitable and natural part of starting out as a new co-creator. There never has been a new co-creator who did not go through this process, what has sometimes been called the "first forgetting." As a co-creator plays many predefined roles and as it is guided by a spiritual teacher, it will ideally begin to overcome this first forgetting. It will begin to realize that it can play many different roles because there is a core of its being that is beyond any role, any form. It will begin to experience glimpses of its pure awareness and its connection to its source.

This will set the foundation for the co-creator reaching the point where it can define its own role and take full responsibility for its life experience. Here is where some co-creators run into trouble that makes them susceptible to dramas. A co-creator is not created to remain in pure awareness, it is created to co-create whereby it expands its sense of self until it reaches the level of the Creator. When you place a new co-creator in a predefined environment, the co-creator cannot remain passive. It must react to its environment, yet in order to react and express itself, it must create a sense of self as a vehicle for dealing with its environment.

The equilibrium effect

In the beginning, this will seem like a chaotic, for some even threatening, process. As a co-creator develops a sense of self, it begins to feel that now it has things more under control. The co-creator develops a sense of equilibrium, and as long as this equilibrium is undisturbed, it feels it can easily deal with life in its environment. What happens to some co-creators – and quite frankly it often happens to the more eager and bright students – is that they eventually develop such an ability to deal with their environment that they feel they have mastery of every aspect of it, meaning they can play any role defined in that environment.

This mastery is genuine, and it indicates that the student is ready to graduate and move on. When the student faces graduation, it suddenly realizes that moving on means that it no longer responds to a predefined environment, but that it now has to define its own environment, its own role, its own life experience. Take note that before this realization, the student had a sense of mastery, meaning it had a sense of equilibrium, feeling it could handle anything in its environment. Now the student realizes that this sense of equilibrium has to go, that its sense of self in its existing environment has to die so that it can be reborn into a new sense of self. This means losing your sense of equilibrium!

This is what I expressed when I said that those who seek to save their lives shall lose them whereas only those who were willing to lose their lives for my sake would attain eternal life. If a co-creator has become attached to its own sense of self and the sense of equilibrium that comes from it, then it will not be willing to give up this known security in order to enter into a new phase with no equilibrium, no sense of security.

This is, of course, perfectly within the Law of Free Will. The co-creator can take another round of playing predefined roles, but as I explained in previous discourses, it cannot stop other co-creators from moving on. A magnetic pull is created by those who do move on, and as it becomes stronger, it becomes more difficult for the remaining co-creators to ignore. The upward pull will begin to disturb the equilibrium of those students who refuse to graduate. That is why they must create a drama that makes it seem like they do not have to graduate and that it is legitimate to resist the upward pull of the Holy Spirit, the River of Life.

This means that any drama that is defined – be it personal or epic – defines a justification for a new sense of equilibrium. The most subtle effect – and in a sense the fundamental "benefit" – of a drama is that it gives those who enter it a sense of equilibrium. The consequence is that the sense of equilibrium is based on the illusions of the drama, which means you are now bound to defend those illusions at all cost. Since the material universe will inevitably challenge all illusions, your life becomes a constant struggle.

Becoming comfortable in the struggle

Even this struggle can give people a sense of equilibrium, as for example Jews and Arabs have found a certain equilibrium in their age-old struggle. The only question is how intense the struggle has to become before you are willing to give up your sense of equilibrium in order to be free of the struggle. The equation is simple. Your attachment to your current sense of equilibrium will determine how hard you are willing to struggle in order to defend the mental box upon which your equilibrium is based. Because of the upward momentum built by others and the second law of thermodynamics, the struggle will inevitably intensify. The only question is how intense it has to become before you have had enough and you are willing to give up your current sense of equilibrium and seek the true peace of the Christ mind.

The situation that the ascended masters face as we attempt to help people escape their dramas is quite simple. The only way we can help people escape their dramas is to challenge the mental box of the drama. People will inevitably experience this as a threat to their sense of equilibrium. This means that those who are the most attached to the sense of equilibrium will resist our efforts with the greatest force. Those who are most in need of help are the least likely to accept our help.

We have now seen why people often cling to their dramas as if it was a matter of life or death. They do this because they have become attached to – addicted to – the sense of equilibrium and security offered by their drama. They feel that if they were to give up their drama – and the world view that makes them think they have the entire universe under control in their mental box – they would die. Of course, their egos would indeed die if they gave up their dramas.

What the epic dramas add to this is that they make people believe that if they gave up the world view that makes them feel they have the universe under control, something bad of epic proportions would happen. For example, the earth or the entire universe would be destroyed or taken over by the devil. Or the devil would take all souls to hell and God's plan for the universe would be sabotaged.

A personal drama ties your sense of equilibrium to what happens in your personal life. The effect of the epic dramas is to tie your sense of equilibrium to what happens in the entire universe. While you may actually be successful in controlling your personal life, you will never be successful in controlling the entire universe (even though some embodied and dis-embodied beings think they can). You are bound to remain unfulfilled indefinitely.

The irony is that a drama is adopted because you are not willing to take full responsibility for your inner circumstances and take control over your life experience regardless of external circumstances. The effect of the drama is to make you believe that your life experience depends on external circumstances. This means that your sense of equilibrium will be dependent upon external circumstances for as long as you are trapped in the drama, which is why you have to try to control your environment, including other people.

If you would only accept full responsibility for your inner situation, you would realize that you have everything you need – right within yourself – to create a true sense of equilibrium. If you think your sense of equilibrium is based on external circumstances, it will be a house built on sand. You may still feel quite secure for a time, but when the rains come, they will wash away your house. If you build your sense of equilibrium on taking command over your inner circumstances, it will be a house built on rocky ground, the rock of Christ. No external circumstances can wash away that house. When you know you are more than anything in this world, how can your sense of self be threatened by anything in this world?

Understanding life and death

I have talked about two basic forces working in this universe:

- There is the force of Life, namely the Holy Spirit or the River of Life. This force is created by those co-creators who have been willing to take responsibility for their life experience and thus attain Christ consciousness, meaning they are constantly transcending themselves, never seeking to hold on to anything.

- There is also the second law of thermodynamics, which does what? It breaks down all organized structures, seeking to return the Ma-ter light to a state where no mental images are superimposed upon it and no forms exist. You might call this the force of death.

Now take this further. We might say that in the – unascended – material universe, the basic force working is the second law, the force of death. As a self-aware being you have two basic options. One is to give in to the force of death and see everything around you be broken down until there is not even a sense of self. The other is to lock in to the River of Life whereby you self-transcend so quickly that you stay ahead of the force of death.

The force of death has a delay factor, a certain speed with which things are broken down. If you transcend your old sense of self faster than the deterioration speed, you will never experience a sense of loss, you will never experience death. The condition is that you cannot hold on to the old sense of self, the old mental box, the old sense of equilibrium. You must be willing to let the old self die, but when you know that you will instantly be reborn into a greater self, you will not experience this as death but as a new birth into something more.

Of course, you also have a third option and that is to resist the force of death. Very few co-creators give in to this force, the majority seek to resist it. How do you resist death? By creating a drama that makes you believe you can actually resist the basic force of the universe. It is precisely the delay factor of the second law that makes dramas possible, as it is possible – for a time – to believe that one can actually resist and that one can hold on to and own something in this world.

Do you grasp the difference between transcending the force of death and resisting this force? If you do, you have started separating yourself from your drama. You can now gain a new perspective on the concept of death. We might say that everything in the material universe is designed to facilitate your growth in self-awareness. This growth can happen in two ways. One is to flow with the River of Life whereby you never have to struggle, never have to resist.

The other is to enter into the consciousness of a drama, which is what I called "death," as when I told the young man to let the dead bury their dead. This can also be called the consciousness of sin or the fall into duality. It has sometimes been called the second forgetting, even the second death—although the "second death" has another meaning as well.

People who enter into a drama set themselves outside the flow of the River of Life, and they automatically and inevitably become subject onto death, to the second law. They will experience the force of death as a threat that is seeking to take away their sense of security and anything they seek to own.

The two forces actually have the exact same aim, namely to facilitate your growth in self-awareness. The River of Life creates an upward pull that disturbs the sense of equilibrium of those in a drama and pulls them higher. The force of death creates a downward pull that seeks to break down the illusions, even the structures, created from the consciousness of the drama. The stark reality is that both forces are designed to set you free from the drama consciousness.

The only real difference is how you respond to life. If you take a positive approach, you join the River of Life and you voluntarily give up your sense of equilibrium, your mental boxes, in order to attain the true peace of the Christ consciousness. If you take a negative approach, you become subject to the force of death that will eventually break down all your mental boxes and your sense of equilibrium until you finally have had enough and give up the attempt to hold on to the equilibrium built on sand.

Either way, you will end up with no mental boxes and both ways can take you to Christ consciousness. One is infinitely harder, for you are creating your own opposition through the images you project into the cosmic mirror, images that are a product of your drama. When you do finally stand naked before God, you will have to choose between going through the second death and be dissolved as a lifestream or starting the path from the point of having nothing. When you choose to flow with the River of Life, you will have to give up the separate self, but you build a timeless self and can continue to expand it.

In a sense, we of the ascended masters could stand back and let the second law do its work, knowing that eventually all would have the opportunity to choose between life and death. Because we have all taken the easier and more joyful way – the strait and narrow way – we desire to offer this way to all. This is why we remain with the earth instead of moving on in the infinite upward spirals that are available to us in the ascended state. We are seeking to inspire you to become part of our upward spiral.

In the next discourse we will consider what the ascended masters can do to help people escape their dramas. We will also discuss what we cannot do and how we must let the laws of the universe be people's teachers.

9 | WHAT THE ASCENDED MASTERS CAN AND CANNOT DO

For thousands of years this planet has been enveloped in a thick cloud created by the epic dramas that where defined by fallen beings who rebelled against God in a higher sphere. These dramas have influenced the thinking of individuals – even entire civilizations – in many subtle ways. When I say "subtle," I mean that the dramas have distorted people's view of life in such a way that people truly and firmly believe that the illusions defined by the dramas are real and give an accurate view of reality. They mistake illusions for reality.

As a result, only very few people in embodiment are able to understand how we of the ascended masters look at the earth and how we seek to help human beings rise above the clouds, the veil, created by the drama consciousness. It is my hope that my discourses on dramas can increase that number.

The grand illusion of right and wrong

Master MORE has said that if people knew better, they would do better. This is true because when the Conscious You truly sees how it is limiting itself, it *will* change. The problem is that the drama consciousness prevents people from actually knowing better. As long as people think their dramas present an accurate view of reality, why would they even consider questioning their dramas, their world view? Why would they even consider that their thought system is simply seeking to fit the entire universe and God into a particular mental box? They will be absolutely convinced that they are doing the right thing, even doing God's work, while they are simply outplaying an epic drama and their personal dramas.

People who are trapped in this state of consciousness cannot fathom that they might be living a lie, they cannot even consider it. How do you know whether you are affected by this subtle lie? Let me give you a guiding rod. I have talked about the Law of Free Will and I have said that this law gives all self-aware beings the right to create any experience they want and to hold on to it for as long as they can. I have said that this law makes you responsible only for your own growth and ascension, but you are not responsible for the growth and ascension of anyone else.

One of the most subtle effects of the consciousness of the epic dramas is the belief that there is an absolute standard for right and wrong. If you follow the standard, you are a good person. If you violate the standard (repeatedly), you are a bad person. Choices can be divided into right and wrong and people can be divided into good and bad. Let me now make an absolute statement. If you believe in this division into right and wrong choices and good and bad people, then you are affected by the epic dramas created by the fallen beings.

There are no two ways about this. We of the ascended masters have ascended precisely because we have transcended all of the epic dramas and their illusions, especially the one just described. We do not evaluate the choices of human beings by comparing them to any standard that can be defined by words and labeling them as right or wrong. We do not evaluate people and label them as good or bad. To us, there are no bad people—but neither are there any good people. We do not look at people and label some as evil, as fallen angels or as beyond hope—even though we are aware of the history of each being.

When we look upon the earth, we see only self-aware beings who are making choices based on their present state of consciousness. To us, the choices you make are irrelevant in the sense that the cosmic mirror will reflect back to you what you send out. We of the ascended masters are not seeking to influence your choices. Why not? Because we understand the eternal truth that your choices are the products of your state of consciousness. We are focused on one thing, namely to inspire you to raise your consciousness. We know that when you do raise your consciousness, your choices will automatically change.

No need to judge others

Here is the problem with the epic dramas. They sprang from the minds of certain beings who came to believe that the fact that co-creators could get lost proved that there was a flaw in the Law of Free Will. These beings reasoned that they had to correct this flaw in God's design by seeking to force other beings to change their choices.

Traditional, mainstream religions on this planet are indeed focused on changing your behavior by making you change the choices you make. What I describe as the outer path is based on the promise that if you change your outer actions – without changing your consciousness, without looking at the beam in your own eye – you can (and will automatically) enter the kingdom.

This is a direct effect of the epic dramas, and it has caused most people to believe in the overall illusion that if only the actions of all people conform to a standard defined by their belief system, then God's kingdom will come to earth. If not, the earth will be destroyed and all souls be captured by the devil. Such people think that it is their duty to change the actions and choices of other people. The net effect being that they look only at the splinters in the eyes of others and do not look at the beam in their own eyes—which means they cannot escape their own dramas and are not growing. They cannot move from the broad way of dramas to the strait and narrow way of Christ.

Consider how subtle and pervasive this state of consciousness is. If you think that you have to "help" other people by getting them – by means that you think are legitimate and benign – to change their minds, change their choices, then you are trapped in an epic drama. If you think you have to evaluate other people's choices and judge them as right or wrong based on any standard, then you are trapped in an epic drama.

We of the ascended masters have no need to judge or evaluate people's choices, as we know a simple reality:

> For by thy words thou shalt be justified, and by thy
> words thou shalt be condemned. (Matthew 12:37)

We also know that this quote is not entirely correct. The true meaning is that by thy WORD thou shalt be justified and condemned. The term WORD refers to a person's total state of consciousness, the sense of self with which you express yourself in this world. This is comparable to the concept of the LOGOS, which is the basic vision – held in the universal Christ mind – that the Creator defined before creating anything that had form. You likewise have a basic vision of life through which you color everything you do in the world of form. This basic vision is shaped by your life experience. I referred to this when I said:

> A good man out of the good treasure of the heart bringeth forth good things: and an evil man out of the evil treasure bringeth forth evil things. (Matthew 12:35)

Obviously, you can see that while in embodiment I did use the dualistic term good and evil, but nevertheless the point is that what I called "the heart" is your WORD, your LOGOS, your basic approach to and outlook upon life in the material world. We might say that entering the kingdom of God, which is the Christ consciousness, is like entering a door with a screen that holds back anything too big to fit through the holes. Any illusions that spring from the duality consciousness – any remnants of a personal or epic drama – cannot pass through the screen and will thus keep the Conscious You from passing through the door as long as you identify with them.

The ascended masters have no need to form opinions, to evaluate or to judge anyone on earth. We know that the law is unfailing and that people will enter the Christ consciousness only when they take full responsibility for their own state of mind instead of worrying about other people's state of mind. We focus all of our attention on inspiring people to raise their consciousness.

In doing so, we are – naturally – having to adapt to people's current state of consciousness. We always have to challenge people's existing mental boxes, but the question is how much we can challenge the mental boxes without disturbing people's sense of equilibrium too much—meaning that they panic, close their minds and start to defend their mental boxes. We walk a delicate balancing act, and let us take a closer look.

The cosmic delay factor

Let us return to the basics. The purpose of life is growth in self-awareness, and the entire world of form is designed to allow a self-aware being to progressively expand its sense of self-awareness from any level to that of a Creator. The vehicle for the expansion of self-awareness is your life experience, the experience you get as you interact with a particular environment in the world of form, including other self-aware beings in that environment.

Your growth in SELF-awareness cannot be forced upon you from without—it must happen as a result of your internal process, meaning how you choose to respond to your environment. You can be put in a situation where you have conditions that make it easier for you to develop self-awareness, but there is no guarantee that all people exposed to the same situation will respond the same way or that all will grow.

What does it mean to grow? It means that you come to the realization that it is not the external circumstances that affect you but your reaction to them that affects you. Your inner life experience is what affects your sense of self, and the master key to your personal growth is to take command over your life experience. The real question is how long it will take for you to come to this realization. However, this can happen only after you have had enough of the experience of allowing external circumstances to control your state of mind. You have the right to have this experience for as long as you want—within the framework of the law.

What is the framework of the law? Since the very purpose is the growth in self-awareness, the law is set up to make sure nothing can stand still. You are either raising your awareness or you are lowering your awareness—there is nothing in between. I know this will seem contradictory to common experience so let me explain. The material universe is in the latest of a series of spheres. Each sphere has been made from progressively denser energies (as its starting point). The denser energies create a delay factor so that it takes time from when a mental image is projected from the mind until the cosmic mirror reflects it back as a physical form/circumstance.

This delay factor is what creates the illusion of time and that you can maintain a certain experience over time. In reality, you are always affected by the two basic forces, namely the force of life (the upward pull) and the force of death (the second law of thermodynamics that seeks to break down any structure). Even though it may seem as if you can maintain certain physical conditions or even a certain inner condition over time, you are always being pulled in one direction or the other, which means your sense of self is either expanding or contracting. You are either flowing with the River of Life and growing, or you are resisting it and thus falling further and further behind, which increases the downward pull.

The two ways to grow

There are two ways to evolve and grow, one is to flow with the River of Life and expand your sense of self and the other is to resist. How can resisting lead to growth? What does growth mean? It means to expand your sense of self, or we might say it means to expand the mental box in which the Conscious You has chosen to clothe itself. When you resist the upward pull, the second law will eventually – and believe me, it *will* happen

– challenge your mental boxes. Growth happens when your mental box is challenged to such an extent that your sense of equilibrium is disturbed. It is important for spiritual students to understand what this means.

The effect of having a sense of equilibrium is that you are not really thinking about life and evaluating your approach to life. You feel that everything is stable and you see no need to rethink your basic approach to life. It is only when your current mental box is challenged to a critical degree that your sense of equilibrium is disturbed to the point where you acknowledge the need to re-evaluate some aspect of your WORD, your LOGOS, your approach to life.

What will it take for a given being to come to the point of acknowledging the need to re-evaluate life? It depends on how attached the being is to its sense of equilibrium. The most advanced students have very little attachment and are constantly re-evaluating some aspect of life, always looking for insights that can help them expand their current mental box—which is seen as simply one step on the staircase of growth. They have taken full responsibility for their state of mind.

Those who are trapped in a drama are very attached to their sense of equilibrium because they stepped into the drama in order to avoid taking responsibility for themselves. They have closed their minds to any knowledge that is beyond the mental box of their drama. Since the mental box is seen as reality, it is believed to be the final view of life—it is a closed system, an end in itself. This means such people are unreachable and unteachable to the true spiritual teachers who have uncompromising respect for free will. These people simply are not on our radar screens, so to speak, as we know the law and physical conditions will take care of their growth. How does this happen? It is what I have called the School of Hard Knocks, and it has three main elements:

•   People are not alone but live in an environment with other people who are trapped in the drama consciousness. Because the epic dramas are defined from the duality consciousness, they always have a built-in conflict. An epic drama is based on a concept of right and wrong and a standard for judging other people as good or bad. It is inevitable that those trapped in one epic drama will see themselves as being in opposition to those trapped in another drama. You see all kinds of groups on earth who are essentially challenging each others mental boxes, and we of the ascended masters really don't need to do anything—people are so good at doing it themselves. The effect of the epic dramas is that you cannot leave other people alone, and this makes sure that everyone's mental box will be challenged by someone.

•   The material universe is designed as a cosmic mirror that reflects back to you what you send out. The Ma-ter light will take on forms that outpicture the mental images projected upon it. As an example, it is the mental images of human beings that have created disease, poverty, starvation and all other limiting conditions on earth. By experiencing such conditions, people's mental boxes can also be challenged to the point where they see the need to re-evaluate their approach to life.

•   The Ma-ter light will take on any form projected upon it, but the second law of thermodynamics will instantly begin to break down any form and return the Ma-ter light to a state of equilibrium. This also works in terms of people's mental boxes, as the second law works only in closed systems. Because of the two factors described above, people begin to defend their mental boxes and close their minds to new knowledge. As soon as their minds become closed systems, the second law begins to create disorder and chaos internally, and this can eventually lead to such stress and mental disease that people can no longer stand it and become willing to rethink.

The School of Hard Knocks

The School of Hard Knocks inevitably leads to suffering. It is really only a matter of how much suffering people are willing to take before they decide to rethink their lives. People create their own suffering by their own resistance to growth—the harder the resistance, the more intense the suffering. It is only a matter of time before people cannot maintain their sense of equilibrium. As their mental boxes are challenged, people do get an opportunity to look at life without the filter of the mental boxes.

The effect is that even though people have been going deeper and deeper into the drama consciousness, they can – at any time – come to the point of being willing to rethink life. If they truly are willing to look beyond their mental box, they can have a true conversion experience that in an instant puts them on the upward path.

We of the ascended masters do not condemn people for taking this road, for we know that even the via dolorosa can lead to genuine growth. Growth means that the dramas are transcended, and you can do that in two ways. You can use a spiritual teaching to see through the illusions of the dramas or you can live out the dramas to the fullest until you have had enough of the struggle and see through them—finally taking responsibility for your life experience. Either way works, and one is not necessarily better than the other. Most self-aware beings have to experience some drama in order to truly gain the experience that empowers them to see through the drama consciousness in all of its forms.

To us, the difference is that those who take the School of Hard Knocks are not open to direct assistance from us, which means we leave them alone and let the law do its work. Only when someone is open to ideas beyond their mental box, do we step in and get more directly involved in helping people grow.

As a matter of completeness, it should be mentioned that the School of Hard Knocks can cause some beings to go into a state of perpetually refusing to rethink. As soon as one mental box is broken down, they create another one that justifies why they do not have to take responsibility for themselves. Because everything in the world of form must have a limit, each lifestream has a given time-span to choose the upward path. If a lifestream refuses, it will go through what has been called the final judgment. In this process, a lifestream is shown all of its mental boxes and illusions so that it can clearly see beyond them. It is then given a choice between taking responsibility for itself (beginning the upward path) or losing its opportunity whereby the Conscious You returns to the I AM Presence and is no longer a self-aware extension, an individualized being.

Seeking to help people through spiritual teachings

I have said that we do not judge people based on a dualistic standard, but we do – naturally – evaluate people. Our criterion is simple: Can we help people or can we not help them? Most people on earth are still in the School of Hard Knocks, and such people simply are not on our radar screen, as they are not open to our help. What will it take for people to be open to us?

In the most general sense, people become open to our help when they reach a critical point of being willing to question their mental boxes even if it disturbs their sense of equilibrium. This might happen as a result of people receiving such hard knocks that their mental boxes and sense of equilibrium are disturbed by force. Or it might happen by people using the mind's built-in ability to analyze and compare whereby they see contradictions in traditional or mainstream thought systems. It might also happen as a result of people developing a love for something more than the dramas.

As I have said, all larger or mainstream thought systems – be they religious, political or scientific – have been influenced by the drama consciousness. They have all become tools for promoting the epic drama that those in a specific thought system are the good people who are working for the ultimate cause, and this gives these people a firm sense of equilibrium. Only when people – one way or another – become willing to question the mental boxes defined by established thought systems, will they be open to direct teachings from us.

What I am talking about here are teachings that are given for a general audience and are available for anyone to find and study. Examples are the teachings of the Buddha, the teachings I gave 2,000 years ago and the teachings we have given through various messengers over the past century.

Consider the reality that we of the ascended masters face. Contrary to what some students prefer to think (based on the drama consciousness) we are not seeking to bring forth an ultimate or absolute teaching. We realize that no teaching expressed in words can be absolute or ultimate. Your Conscious You has the capacity to experience ultimate truth – what I called the Spirit of truth – but only by going beyond any expression in the world of form and experiencing its source, the Creator.

We are practical realists who are seeking to reach as many people as possible, meaning we inspire or release many different teachings. Each teaching is carefully adapted to a group of people who are affected by a particular epic drama or mental box. In order for such a teaching to be successful, the first requirement is that it must contain something that the people can fathom and relate to with their present state of consciousness.

Even a teaching given by us must be adapted to people's mental box, which means that it can be necessary for us to seemingly confirm certain illusions to which the people we seek to reach are attached. In order to reach people, we cannot challenge their mental box beyond what their sense of equilibrium can deal with. If we give a teaching that is too far beyond people's mental box, we cannot reach them at all, and thus we cannot even begin to help them. Our teachings are not given in order to set forth ultimate truth. They are given in order to offer a specific group of people a way to transcend a particular mental box—and once they have done that then connect to the ongoing path.

Many of the teachings we give and inspire are given for people who are not ready to acknowledge the existence of ascended masters so we keep our identity secret. There is a great variety of such teachings, often disguised as self-help or as belonging to a particular tradition. For example, we must take vastly different approaches in order to help people from a Christian, a Muslim or a Buddhist background.

Within the last century, we have also sponsored certain teachings that openly spoke about us and that sought to give forth a more universal teaching for people who had attained a higher degree of openness. Even such teachings are not meant to set forth an ultimate truth. Up until now, our teachings have all been designed to help people escape the mental boxes of the Piscean age, which means they had to be adapted to those mental boxes to some degree. Even the teachings given by us as direct revelation have been adapted to people's mental boxes, including the epic dramas that dominated the Piscean age.

This realization has many ramifications, but the one I want to focus on here is the fact that people who find these teachings respond to them based on their personal and epic dramas, their mental boxes. The teachings have been published for anyone to find, and the only real criteria is people's willingness to question their mental boxes. The important question is how this willingness came about.

Most people on earth have enrolled themselves in the School of Hard Knocks. For some the knocks eventually became so hard that they developed a willingness to question certain mental boxes. The crucial distinction is that for most people this did not mean that they also developed a willingness to take responsibility for themselves. Take note that people can indeed develop this willingness through the School of Hard Knocks, but the fact that they are in this school proves that at one point they refused to take full responsibility. They have a big hurdle to overcome and must go through a change of heart.

The vast majority of the people who have – over the past century and more – found a teaching sponsored by the ascended masters have come in without the willingness to take full responsibility for themselves. We have been fully aware of this, and our teachings have been designed to help people take that responsibility. We have also been fully aware that there is no way to guarantee that people will actually accept responsibility.

It is quite possible to be willing to question your mental boxes in terms of questioning outer teachings or thought systems without being willing to look in the mirror and take responsibility for yourself. For example, many people can clearly see the fallacy of mainstream religion, and they are quick to place blame upon various external sources who supposedly tricked them and other people. However, an illusion can only appeal to you if you have something in your own consciousness that corresponds to that illusion. That something is a spiritual blindness that prevents you from seeing through the illusion. Where does spiritual blindness come from? It comes from your unwillingness to look at yourself in the mirror, which comes from your unwillingness to take full responsibility for your state of mind.

Misusing our teachings to build an equilibrium

A majority of the people who come into ascended master teachings are willing to question their mental boxes but are not – yet – willing to take responsibility for themselves. I have talked about your mental box and your sense of equilibrium. For this discussion, the mental box is how you look at the world, including an outer religion you follow. It is how you *look out from* yourself. Your sense of equilibrium is how you look at yourself, meaning how you *look in at* yourself.

As an example, let us take a person who grew up in a mainstream Christian religion. He eventually receives some hard knocks that cause him to acknowledge the contradictions of his belief system. He is willing to question his outer religion, his mental box. As a result of this, he finds the ascended masters' teachings and it opens his mind further. He comes to reason that his traditional religion was influenced by the power elite and dark forces, and he places all responsibility on these external forces. What he has not done is look at what it was in his consciousness that caused him to be born in that environment—what it is he needs to learn about his approach to life and religion in order to rise above his current level of consciousness. He has not yet taken responsibility for himself but is placing responsibility outside himself. While this may still lead to a growth in his understanding of the world, it has not yet led to a growth in his state of consciousness.

Another way to say this is that such a person has had his mental box challenged, but he has not yet had his sense of equilibrium challenged so severely that he is willing to look at himself. Most of the people who find our teachings either have their sense of equilibrium largely intact or have only had it challenged to some degree. This – finally – brings us to the point I want to make with this discussion.

Most of our students come to our teachings with a desire to reinforce or repair their sense of equilibrium. They quickly take our teachings and build a new sense of equilibrium, which means they have now used our teachings to justify why they do not need to look at themselves!

They have taken an ascended master teaching and elevated it to some ultimate status, such as claiming it is the most advanced teaching on the planet or the gospel for the next 2,000 years. They have selected certain aspects of the teaching and used them to build a sense that they have no need to truly question their basic approach to life and religion. After all, since they have found and accepted this advanced teaching – as opposed to the majority who are not evolved enough to accept the teaching – they must be advanced students. As such, they have no need to even consider that they have a beam in their own eyes.

As a result, their minds become closed systems. We of the ascended masters cannot reach them, even though they claim to be our best students and call upon us day and night. We can only stand by and say to them (which they cannot hear):

"Hello, if you want to see us, look inside yourself. When you have been willing to look at and see through anything that is in there, you will see us on the other side!"

The self-esteem trap

Why is it that people need a sense of equilibrium? All self-aware beings need some foundation for their interaction with their environment, some sense of who they are. A new co-creator who is playing a role gets this sense of identity from the role he or she is playing, and it gives a sense of self-esteem.

As you come to the turning point of having to take responsibility, you awaken from the first forgetting. You now reconnect to the fact that the core of your being is the Conscious You, which is an extension of the Creator's own Being. You also become aware of your I AM Presence, and thus you begin to know your spiritual individuality—as opposed to the sense of self you have built as a result of playing roles in your environment.

The importance is that you gain the best possible foundation for developing true self-esteem, namely that you realize that you are a spiritual being who is beyond any role you have played in this world and beyond any self you have developed in this world. The only true source of self-esteem is to recognize that you are an extension of the Creator's Being—and that all other self-aware beings are also extensions of the same source. It is a self-esteem that is beyond and thus independent of anything in this world.

How do you develop this self-esteem? There is only one way. You must take full responsibility for yourself. You must realize that it is your responsibility to connect to your inner being and that you must never allow anything in this world to come between you and your source. You must take full responsibility for being in command of your state of mind, regardless of anything that happens in this world.

When you do this, you realize that your Conscious You is more than any other sense of self you have developed in this world; it is more than any sense of self based on the illusion of separation or the consciousness of duality. As such, you have the potential to transcend, to rise above, to leave behind any lesser self and begin to express your spiritual individuality in this world. You can come to the point where your sense of self – the self you use as a vehicle for self-expression in this world – is in complete alignment with the individuality in your I AM Presence. You are here below all that you are Above.

What happens when a lifestream refuses to take this full responsibility? It goes into the drama consciousness, and that means it accepts a dualistic illusion as a justification for not looking at itself. It now builds a sense of self-esteem – a sense of equilibrium – on this illusion, and as I have explained above, any illusion will inevitably be challenged in the School of Hard Knocks. You now have a being who is in a constant struggle to build, secure and defend its self-esteem, its sense of equilibrium.

On an even deeper level, the unwillingness to take responsibility for yourself makes a being vulnerable to the epic dramas. The reason is that the epic dramas seemingly offer an easy way out of the self-esteem problem. These dramas – in any number of different variations – define a thought system that divides people into two categories, those who are good and those who are bad. By entering into this consciousness, you take over the basic belief that there is an absolute right and wrong – as defined by your belief system – and that it is perfectly justified to judge people and label them.

You enter the "us versus them" mentality and the advantage it offers you (when you are not willing to take responsibility for yourself) is that by merely belonging to the good people, you have a foundation for self-esteem. You are part of the group of people who are not only good, but who are actually fighting for the victory of God's plan on earth and for the defeat of those who oppose God. What better foundation for self-esteem could you have—in this world.

All are affected by epic dramas

The illusions of the epic dramas have been so intricately woven into the fabric of consciousness on this planet that it is virtually impossible to grow up without being affected by them. What are we of the ascended masters to do when we give forth a new teaching? We have to give something that appeals to people and also is in line with the lessons people have to learn at the time. One of the main lessons humanity was meant to learn in the Age of Pisces was precisely to overcome the epic dramas. This explains why our previous teachings have contained certain elements that are clearly dualistic and adapted to the epic mindset.

Each of our previous teachings has been a calculated risk. We know very well that most people – the vast majority – who find our teachings are affected by the epic mindset and have built their self-esteem on its illusions. We know it is inevitable that such people will use our teachings to reinforce their sense of self-esteem, their sense of equilibrium, based on the belief that they are the good people and that they are on the side of ultimate good.

We cannot require that people leave behind their epic dramas before they enter the door—as that would defeat the purpose for giving a teaching. If people had already transcended the epic mindset, they would not need an external teaching as we could work with them directly within themselves. Those who do need an outer teaching are guaranteed to be in the epic mindset, and we must adapt the teaching to this fact. This means that we must cater to the need that people have, including the need to feel special because they have found the teaching.

There is no way around this. It is a practical reality that we who are above the fallen consciousness must work within the framework defined by the fallen beings. If it is likely that the teaching will reinforce the epic mindset and the false self-esteem, does that not defeat the purpose from the very beginning? Not necessarily, because we have options for helping people transcend the epic mindset once they have walked through the door. For those who can read between the lines of any previous teaching – for those who have eyes to see – there are innumerable clues that can help people see beyond the epic mindset.

Of course, there is no guarantee that people will see or internalize these clues. The majority of ascended master students will not and have not used our teachings to transcend the epic mindset. However, are they any worse off than if they had stayed in any other thought system that reinforces this mindset?

We always have the initiation faced by Gautama Buddha as he had entered Nirvana and contemplated returning to earth in order to teach what he had discovered. The temptation was that the difference between the state of consciousness he had attained and the state of consciousness of most people on earth was so great that no one would be able to understand his teaching. He overcame that temptation by stating the eternal truth guaranteed by the upward momentum of this sphere as a whole: "Some will understand."

For each teaching we have given, some have understood and have bridged the gap between their epic mental box and the ascended consciousness. I am hoping that by talking about these topics in a more direct manner than has ever been done before, even more will understand and rise above.

❧

The essence of a drama is
that you think the fulfillment
of your goals in life
(even your salvation)
depends on the choices
made by other people.

❧

10 | PLAY YOUR PART—
INDEFINITELY

NOTE: This discourse was given as a spoken dictation in front of an audience whereas the other discourses were written.

Jesus: Shakespeare, who was an embodiment of Saint Germain, coined the immortal words: "All the world's a stage." I would add that all the world's a stage—in which all the roles are defined by the fallen beings. I have said that in order for you to step onto the path of Christhood, you have to be willing to start defining your own role on earth instead of playing predefined roles. You especially have to stop playing the roles that the fallen beings have defined for human beings.

This is truly a challenge because the effect of the epic dramas is that the fallen beings have defined a large number of roles that are not seen as roles. Instead, they are seen as being real and as being mandated by God. The message being that you must continue to play these roles until the end of your life or until the epic objective has been achieved—which, as I have explained, will never happen. Many people are trapped in playing these roles—indefinitely. Consider how easy it has been for the fallen beings to pull people into the epic dramas. All they have to do is to commit some kind of aggressive act against someone, and if that someone feels violated – feels victimized, feels attacked, feels unjustly treated – then that person will slip into the dualistic mindset and will then play the role of one of the dualistic identities that have been created over time.

Playing a pre-defined role

The beings who fell in the higher spheres created certain identities based on duality. These identities can be compared to the roles you have in a theater production where some people play the hero, some people play the villain, some people play the victims. Those who are trapped in duality are already – without realizing it – trapped in one of these dualistic identities, in one of these parts, one of these roles in the play.

When they act out that role in aggression against the innocents who are not yet trapped in such a role, there is a possibility – a strong possibility – that the innocent children will feel victimized by the aggressor and therefore will slip into the role of being a victim. Then they are trapped in the dualistic dramas of the ego. Now they see themselves in relation to – in opposition to – someone else who is in a dualistic role. Without knowing it, they slip right into one of these dualistic roles, such as the role of victim. Some slip into another role, that of the one who seeks revenge, or that of the one who seeks justice by somehow compensating for the wrongs done in the past by committing another wrong in the present.

This is the basic fabric of the ego—that it always plays one of these dualistic roles, it takes on one of these dualistic identities. You need to become wise as serpents so that you can see the unreality of the serpentine mind, the serpentine logic, that has created these varied dualistic parts and identities. You can then realize that you have taken this on as an actor in the theater takes on a costume, puts on make-up, puts on false teeth or a wig or a hump on the back in order to resemble the part it is meant to play.

When you see the unreality of this, when you become wise as a serpent – wise to the serpents – you realize that you are not the part you are playing, you are more than that part. That is when you can begin to contemplate the possibility of separating yourself from the part, even separating yourself from the entire play so that you can eventually walk out of the theater and say: "I have had enough of playing that old worn-out part. Find somebody else, for you will have to do without me. I am done with this. I have had enough!"

The game ends when you decide to stop playing

When will your struggles end? You have free will, do you not? When will your struggles end? When you decide that they will end, *now!* Can you make that decision right now? Perhaps not. But I tell you, there will come a now when you can make that decision—if you decide that it is going to happen *now*.

The universe is a mirror, which means that whatever you send out, the universe must reflect back. When you take on a certain role in the play, in the dualistic play, then the universe thinks that you want to experience the outer conditions that correspond to the role. If you feel like a victim of life or a victim of outer circumstances, the subconscious message you are sending into the cosmic mirror is that you want to experience what it is like to be a victim. The more victimized you feel, the more frustrated you feel, the universe can interpret that in only one way: "Oh, he wants to experience even more of a struggle, he wants to be victimized even more."

Why does the universe interpret it that way? Because the cosmic mirror has absolute respect for your free will. As long as you are in that role, that identity of being the victim, the universe can only interpret it in one way, namely that you are not done playing the part of a victim. You still want to experience what it is like to be a victim. Naturally, the universe gives you what you want. It will continue to do so, even accelerating it, until you finally come to the point where you take responsibility and say: "Okay. I have been a victim for a long time, but it was because I made a decision that caused me to enter into that victim consciousness. I took on that part, I put on that costume. But I have had enough of it!" You then decide that you will no longer play that part.

Let me assure you that the universe is based on free will, which means that whenever you decide you have had enough, you are free to leave the theater. Even if it is the night before the big premiere, you are free to quit and say: "Enough of this madness!" This is why you need to be wise as a serpent. Because the serpents will do everything they can to make you believe in the lie that for this, that or the next reason you cannot just walk out of here, you cannot just walk out of that part. Once you have taken it on, it is permanent, you can never escape—or so they want you to believe.

This is why they have come up with so many clever illusions, including the mainstream Christian delusion that you cannot save yourself but that only Jesus, as the external savior, can save you. All of these Christians think they are headed straight for heaven. But they are still in the consciousness of being a victim, still feeling that there is some external force who is pulling them down to hell or pulling them up to heaven—when in reality it is themselves and their own consciousness that is pulling them up or down. Where your treasure is, there will your heart be also (Matthew 6:21).

The ego cannot become harmless as a dove

The ego will always be locked in this dualistic drama of playing a part where it is either the aggressor and villain, or the victim, or the hero, or some other role that is part of this battle between opponents, between two sides. Most people on earth and most religions on earth have fallen victim to this consciousness. Even though one can say that there is an epic struggle between good and evil, the way the world looks at that struggle is false because it is influenced by the dualistic consciousness that has turned the struggle between good and evil into a dualistic one. No matter which part you play in that struggle, you are only serving to perpetuate the struggle itself and keep yourself stuck in that struggle.

We now come to the second part of my statement, for when you become wise as a serpent – you realize what is going on, you realize the dualistic game – then you can fulfill the second requirement and become harmless as a dove (Matthew 10:16). As long as you think you have to eradicate evil, you are simply trapped in the dualistic game. As long as you think you have to serve the external God in the sky – and as long as your religious quest is based on the desire to serve the external God rather than serving the internal God that is in all life – you are still part of the struggle.

The only way to escape the struggle is to become harmless as a dove by letting go of all desire for justice, for revenge, for somehow making up for old wrongs by committing new wrongs. The only way out is through unconditional surrender, unconditional love. Sometimes people – in the most tense life-threatening situations – instead of fighting it, instead of resisting it, instead of feeling victimized, they simply surrender. In that surrender they become harmless as a dove. In that surrender they possess their lives.

The Holy Spirit, often depicted as a dove, may then descend and change the situation so that what seems to be the guaranteed outcome may not come to pass. Because somehow – by the person who is cast to be in the role of the victim refusing to play the role of the victim – the person that is trapped in the role of the aggressor is empowered to see beyond the role and realize that he too is more than the part he is playing. He does not need to act out that part in all the grizzly detail that was in the script written by the fallen beings.

Set everyone free by refusing to play the part

By you refusing to play your part in the dualistic struggle, you might inspire others to realize that there is an alternative, there is a way beyond the struggle, there is something beyond the struggle, there is more to life than the dualistic struggle. This, of course, is the essence of my teaching and my example. If you truly look at my life based on the understanding I have just given, you will see that I too refused to play the part that I had been assigned. I refused to live up to the expectations of the Jews for what the Messiah should be like.

Look at the scribes and Pharisees who wanted me to fit into the mental box they had created, based on the old scriptures, based on their tradition. They used their tradition to create an expectation of exactly how the Messiah should play his part. They thought that the Living Christ – when he came to earth – would slip right into one of the dualistic roles in the play and would find his part in the dualistic play. If I had lived up to their dualistic expectations, I would have confirmed those dualistic expectations. How could I have had any chance of helping them rise above those limitations?

When the Living Christ appears on earth, his first and foremost task is to refuse to fit into any of the dualistic roles created in the theater production called earth, in the drama, in the classic tragedy called earth—or for that matter the comedy. Really, when you look at earth you have to say: "Things are so bad you have to either laugh or cry." Some will prefer to cry, and some will prefer to laugh.

The Living Christ must stand back from it all and say: "I am not here to confirm people's illusions, I am here to challenge them!" You challenge them only when you refuse to play the part that they have assigned to you—whatever that part may be, be it your family, your society, your religion. It is impossible to grow up on earth without growing up in an environment where there is someone or some institution that has a preassigned role for you that they desperately want you to fit into.

The challenge for all spiritual people is to free yourself from that programming, to free yourself from the roles that you have been brought up to play in this lifetime – or that you have played in previous lifetimes – that have caused you to build certain beliefs and programs in the subconscious mind that are still there, haunting you. Because you think you have to play that part, you still think you have to act out that role, whatever it may be.

Recognizing the more subtle parts

It might be easy to see that playing the aggressor, playing the villain is a dualistic part. It may even be easy to see that being a victim is a dualistic part. But how many are able to see that even playing the hero is a dualistic part? This is a special challenge. Many spiritual people have descended from above on a rescue mission. They have come here to be the prince on the white horse that rides into town and frees the people from the bad guys.

Unfortunately, through movies and popular culture even *that* has been turned into a dualistic part where the hero is cast in the role of him who fights the villain. That is not the way to truly free the people from duality. There were many Jews who expected the Messiah to be one of the warrior kings of the Old Testament and lead them in an uprising against the Romans. Many of them rejected me when I refused to play that part.

It is subtle to see through the dualistic parts that have been created in order to trap you indefinitely in the dualistic game. It takes discernment. Where will that discernment come from? It will come from only one place—the Living Word, the Christ consciousness.

Ponder this simple question: "Do I like the part I am currently playing in the drama on earth?" If you do not, I tell you, you are free to walk out of it at this very moment. As I said 2,000 years ago: "The kingdom of God is at hand," meaning that it is an option that is available to you right now and will be available to you at any moment in the future.

I recommend that you do not misunderstand the concept of the Eternal now, thinking it means you have eternity to make the decision to let go of the old and leave the part you have been playing. After all, you are in a world of time and space so there is no eternity in this realm.

You are an actor in a cosmic play, and you can take off the make-up, you can take off the costume, you can take off the humpback, you can take off the wig, you can take off the big nose and the crooked teeth and throw them all in the garbage bin as you walk out of the theater, saying: "Goodbye and good riddance, for I have understood the meaning of Jesus' words: 'What is that to thee, follow thou me.'"

11 | COULD GOD MAKE A MISTAKE?

One aspect of my role as a spiritual teacher is to stir you into action, to give you an energetic impulse that can help you rise above your normal state of awareness and decide to embark on a new phase of your path to Christhood. This path has both evolutionary and revolutionary phases, and sometimes you do truly need to awaken to a new realization that helps you make a decision to rise to a new level. That is what I sought to do in the previous discourse.

Once you have risen to a new level, you will, of course, face the evolutionary challenge of dealing with the initiations of that level. Hopefully, I have now helped you see the need to rise to the level where you are consciously dealing with the epic dramas, and in the following discourses I will give you the insights that will empower you to transcend these dramas.

The epic dramas have had major physical consequences on this planet, but the most devastating effect is that they present you with an enigma, a riddle that is difficult to solve. This is what causes many people to either accept the dramas and seek to outplay them or to become so overwhelmed by the dramas that they are spiritually paralyzed. Just look at the story of the temptation of Eve where Eve was cast into doubt by the serpentine logic.

The epic dramas distort the way people look at every aspect of life and they do so in a way that is very difficult for most lifestreams to deal with. New co-creators simply don't have the self-awareness to deal with the questions posed by the epic dramas. That is why they are often paralyzed by doubt and cannot reason against the serpentine logic presented in the dramas. They have not become wise as serpents, and that makes it very difficult to become harmless as doves.

As you step onto the path to Christhood, you must start to deal with the serpentine illusions and overcome them one by one. You must become wise as serpents while becoming completely non-violent and overcoming all desire to use force. In order to reach the highest level of Christhood, you must overcome each and every serpentine illusion. This truly must be done through Christ discernment that can only come from inside yourself. Your ability to reason can be a valuable tool for getting started on the process of building Christ discernment. To that end, I will give you some insights in order to help you sharpen your reasoning ability and your discernment. Let us reason together.

The difference between true and false teachers

As a new co-creator you have only a limited self-awareness and you are simply not ready to deal with large or cosmological questions. As you grow in self-awareness, you will expand your ability to deal with such questions. You will also be guided by your spiritual teacher to deal with each and every question related to life, God and the universe. However, take note of an important difference.

The true spiritual teacher is not in duality and has no personal need to control you or convince you that a certain viewpoint is right. Such a teacher will present you with the Christ reality about a certain topic or question. He or she will start by letting you make your own decision and will then give you teachings or ask you questions aimed at guiding you towards a higher understanding. If you want an example of how a teacher might work, consider the Greek Philosopher Socrates who asked questions in order to get people to question what they took for granted.

The true teacher has no need to get you to accept any particular view because the real aim is to raise your self-awareness, which can happen only through your own internal processes. The true teacher has no agenda and simply seeks to stimulate your internal process without controlling it or working towards a particular outcome. Contrary to what many people believe, the aim of a true teacher is not to get you to accept certain facts or dogmas but to raise your level of self-awareness. Furthermore, the true teacher never directs any forceful or aggressive energy at you. Why is this so? Because the true teacher has personally resolved all questions and knows that God's plan for the universe works perfectly. He works within that plan and sees no need to correct it.

In contrast, the false teachers believe there is a fundamental flaw in God's design. They have various specific ways of describing this flaw, as we will see, yet the true "flaw" they do not like is that all self-aware beings were created equal, meaning that God did not put them in charge of the universe. They wanted to rule their original sphere and have special status and privileges. When they were not allowed to, they rebelled and have ever since tried to prove God wrong by getting other beings to misuse their free will. They have also tried to set themselves up in this world with the power and privileges they so strongly crave. As a result of this, they do have a clear agenda, and it is not to raise your self-awareness. It is to get you to unknowingly limit your self-awareness so you never manifest and express your Christhood on earth. Christianity is simply a mind-control machine designed to make sure that there will never be another person doing the works that I did.

The main mode of the false teachers is that they seek to deceive you and cast doubt upon everything. You may say that Socrates also raised doubt about everything, but the difference was in both intention and method. It is one thing to ask questions that make people think, it is another thing to accuse people that what they believe is wrong according to some epic standard. It is one thing to encourage people to expand their awareness, it is another to seek to get them to accept one particular viewpoint—especially when that viewpoint springs from the mind of anti-christ.

The main difference is that a true teacher is energetically non-aggressive. He or she never directs any aggressive or force-based energy at you. The true teacher gives you knowledge and insights or asks questions, but there is no lower energy that turns them into arrows that force their way into your energy field. In contrast, the false teachers create a psychic impulse made up of two elements. One is a particular lie based on serpentine logic, and the other is an energy impulse charged with lower emotions, such as fear, doubt, anger, blame etcetera.

The true teacher accepts your mind as your exclusive domain. The false teacher has no such respect and is constantly seeking to force its way into your mind for the purpose of causing it to become paralyzed into blind acceptance of a certain epic drama. You can actually learn to expose the false teachers by reading the vibration of the intention behind what they say or write. You can even learn to read the vibration of an idea. This is all part of Christ discernment.

Again, why were the fallen beings allowed to embody on earth? Because a critical mass of the original inhabitants had gone into duality whereby they had become lost to the true teachers. This meant they could learn only from the School of Hard Knocks, but even this school has teachers. Only, the teachers are the fallen beings who seek to force the minds of the students. One could say that after so many lifestreams entered duality, the Karmic Board who oversees the evolutions of earth decided that if people truly wanted to learn from the School of Hard Knocks, they would allow the fallen beings to embody here. The purpose was to make the knocks harder in order to shorten the time it would take before lifestreams began to question whether there might not be a higher way to learn.

We could therefore say that the fallen beings are substitute teachers. Of course, they are not seeking to help you learn or raise your awareness. They are seeking to keep you under their control. This does not mean that you cannot learn from the false teachers. However, you will not learn as long as you are allowing them to manipulate your mind. You will learn from them only when you become aware of their existence and learn to see through the illusions they use in order to manipulate your mind. You will not learn by listening to them; you will learn only when you stop listening to them.

Helping you to stop listening to the false teachers is the role of a true teacher so let me get on with my job.

Has something gone wrong with God's design?

Mainstream Christianity presents the classical epic drama, namely that God's plan for the salvation of the universe is threatened by the devil who is working to take all souls to hell. This would then cause God to destroy the world. In order to prevent this, God sent his only begotten son – me – to the world and those who accept me and the Christian religion will be saved. I will, supposedly, return to earth at some future date, defeat the devil and establish God's kingdom on earth. In order to help me do this, human beings need to give God a hand in defeating the devil, which has been used to justify various violent acts, such as the Inquisition, the Crusades and others.

Let us now step back from this scenario and consider what is the – unspoken and for most people unrecognized – claim behind this epic drama. It is generally claimed by the Christian religion that God is almighty and all good. The epic scenario makes the implicit claim that this almighty and good God somehow made a mistake when he created the world. How else can you explain that souls can be lost and that the devil could take the earth to a point where God might have no other option than to destroy it?

Let us now consider a question that for many Christians would be close to blasphemy. If God really is perfect, all-powerful and all-knowing, could God actually have made a mistake? How could a supposedly perfect God create a world that is obviously so imperfect?

In order to approach this question, let us start by considering why the unspoken claim behind the epic scenario seems plausible to human beings. We first have the fact that new co-creators simply do not have the self-awareness to deal with such large-scale questions. When the fallen beings first came to this planet, the co-creators who had gone into duality – and who had therefore lost the direct guidance of the ascended masters – simply did not have the wisdom to refute the claims made by the fallen beings. As seen with Eve in the Garden, their minds were paralyzed by the serpentine logic. Another factor is that, as I have explained, there are two groupings of fallen beings. There are those who very openly and aggressively attack human beings and seek to force them into submission and brutally destroy those who will not submit.

The brutality and viciousness displayed by the fallen beings when they first embodied on earth was something that human beings had never encountered before. Although humans had gone into duality, they had never fought each other with such disrespect for life as displayed by the fallen beings. These beings quickly set themselves up as leaders, and they caused societies to go to war against each other. Fighting on the scale of war was unprecedented on earth and it was indeed a group of fallen beings who taught human beings to wage war. By observing the brutality taking place on earth, human beings were so shocked that they grappled for an explanation.

A second group of fallen beings now stepped in, and they were the "wiser" ones who came up with the epic scenario in order to explain the behavior of the first group of fallen beings. Indeed, the explanation was that there is a force, personified as the ultimate brutal being, who is opposing God. This force is influencing the people who are opposing our society, and in order to save the earth, it is necessary that we defeat the evil people. Doing this is necessary in order to fulfill God's plan. It is mandated and justified by God that we become as brutal as our opponents, even more brutal so we can defeat them.

The effect of separation

This is a true and accurate description of why human beings started believing in the epic scenario. One group of fallen beings provided the outer demonstration and another group of fallen beings provided the ideological framework. This is not the full explanation because it leaves out the psychological component. Without understanding the psychological perspective, you will never reach personal Christhood. The reason being, of course, that everything revolves around the psychology of individual beings.

I have in the previous discourses (in this and the two other ego books) given teachings about separation, and we now need to put them together. I have said that when you go into separation, it is difficult for the Conscious You to experience pure awareness. You cannot experience directly that God is formless. As a co-creator who has not gone into separation, you constantly experience that you have to deal with a world where everything has form. You can never fully identity yourself with this world – and the outer self you have created to deal with it – because you have some sense of the formless.

When you lose this sense of the formless, all you experience is form. It therefore becomes self-evident to the new separate you, the Unconscious You, that even God must have a form. You might recall that Genesis says God created man in his image and after his likeness. When the Unconscious You was created, it immediately started creating a God in its own image and after its own – form-based – likeness. In this respect it truly does not matter what form God takes. It is a God who has form and thus not the formless God. What is the difference? A formless God can be manipulated by the form-based self whereas the formless God can never be confined to or manipulated by anything in the world of form.

When the fallen beings came to earth, human beings had various conceptions of God or gods. Most of these were what today's religions call primitive, such as gods in nature or a God who was a kind of magician that would fulfill the wishes of those who performed certain acts (prayers, sacrifices etcetera).

What the fallen beings did was to impose their own self-created image of God upon human beings, seeking to get all people to believe in their various images of a god. This god created by the fallen beings had one overall characteristic, namely that he had a form that could be opposed by another form. It did not really matter what particular form was taken by God and his opponent, and the fallen beings would use whatever a group of people already believed in. What mattered was that the new god had an opponent and therefore the world was locked in an epic struggle between good and evil. Before the arrival of the fallen beings, this concept was completely unknown to human beings. They simply did not have the concept of a God who could be opposed by anything. Why would they have a concept of evil when they had never experienced evil?

Now back to the psychological effect. Because people had lost the direct experience of the formless, the Unconscious You found it easy to accept a form-based god. This was made easier by the central feature of the consciousness of separation, namely that you refuse to accept full responsibility for yourself. How can you deny that you have full responsibility for your destiny? You must deny that you have free will. Why did human beings accept the image of God presented by the fallen beings? Because the form-based god offers a major advantage to the Unconscious You. The advantage is that the Conscious You can remain unconscious and thus the Unconscious You can remain alive. How so? Because if God has created the world and if a devil is opposing God, it follows that human beings are caught in the middle of this epic battle. Humans are largely powerless and they have little responsibility.

We now see that those who oppose your group of people can be defined as having been taken over by the devil. This explains why they will not submit to your leader – who is representing God – and this justifies that your side kills the other side. You can now accept that you are a powerless being and blindly follow the blind leaders. This scenario seems completely implausible from the Christ mind. But it seems eminently

plausible when seen from inside the perception filter of a separate mind. The Conscious You does have the ability to step
outside of it, reconnect to pure awareness and see the fallacy
of the epic scenario. The Unconscious You simply has no way
to do this and thus has no defense. Those in separation cannot
avoid being sucked into the epic scenario, and it is really just a
matter of which group of fallen beings they decide to follow.

Did God really make a mistake?

Now that we have seen why people accept the epic scenario,
let us get back to the question. I have explained that the purpose for the entire world of form is that the Creator wants
to create beings who grow into the Creator consciousness.
The Creator creates individual extensions of itself who start
out with a point-like sense of self. They gradually expand that
sense of self until they reach the Creator consciousness.

What most people have not understood is that the process
of expanding your self-awareness is possible only because you
have free will. I fully realize this is a difficult point to get, and
it might require some contemplation. For starters, consider
what it means to be in the Creator consciousness. As a Creator
you can create absolutely any kind of world you can imagine.
You are a completely self-sufficient and independent being,
meaning that nothing restricts your imagination or your ability
to choose what to create. As a Creator you have a will that is
entirely free because nothing restricts or opposes it.

This does not mean that a Creator has no awareness of
consequences. A Creator is fully aware that in order to create
a world of form, certain choices have to be made. You cannot
create a world that is everything at the same time. A world of
form is a world where every form is set apart, and this means
choices were made and these choices have consequences.

Before deciding what kind of world to create, a Creator carefully considers the consequences of its design and chooses accordingly.

Why does a Creator have this awareness of consequences? Because it too started out as a self-aware being inside a world of form defined by another Creator. It worked its way up to the Creator consciousness by exercising its own will and observing the consequences of its choices. (I know the linear mind will ask who created the first world of form and where that first Creator came from, but that question has no answer that the linear mind can grasp. The Conscious You can grasp the answer by experiencing infinite awareness in which no beginning is necessary.)

Without going into a very complex discussion, free will is necessary in order for individual beings to expand their consciousness. You grow by making choices, observing the consequences and then making new choices based on your experience. Once you understand this, you see that God did not make a mistake by giving individual beings free will. Free will is essential to the very purpose of creation. Without free will, creation would be pointless because robotic beings could never be raised to the awareness of a Creator.

We now see a truth that is obvious from the Christ consciousness, namely that God did not make a mistake by giving beings free will. Why does it then seem plausible to so many people that God must have made a mistake?

Understanding free will

What does it truly mean that God has given individual beings a will that is entirely free? We first have to look at the "free" aspect of free will. Only a being who has self-awareness can have any kind of will. I have said that the Conscious You starts out with a point-like sense of self. In reality, you will always have a point-like center of your being. Why? Because truly free choices can be made only from a single point. Only when your awareness is concentrated in a single point will all avenues be open to you.

As an, admittedly inadequate, visual illustration, imagine you are standing in the center of a large open space. Because your body is concentrated in a single location, you can turn freely and walk in any direction you choose. Now imagine that your body is nailed to a large wooden cross. Can you turn easily? Can you move in any direction you choose?

We now need to consider the connection between free will and self-awareness. In the previous book I gave a discourse in which I talk about choice versus selection. I would like to insert this here:

Choice versus selection

Let me try to illustrate this with a linear (thus not entirely adequate) image. The material world is finite, meaning that although you can choose to create many different selves, there is a limit to what can be created (at least on this one planet). Let us say that in the very beginning, the Conscious You is standing in the center of a circle. As you know, the circle is a symbol for infinity because it seemingly has no beginning and no end. We can turn the circle into a symbol for the material world by dividing it into a circumference with 360 degrees or angles.

Imagine that you are standing in a single point that is the center of a circle. The circle has 360 degrees on the circumference, which means you can draw a pie-like figure where each degree forms a triangular shape. You are the Conscious You in its singular or centered stage. You can choose to go into any of the 360 different kinds of selves available in your circle in order to experience what it is like to look at the material world through that self.

Now imagine that you pick one self and the triangular shape can be compared to a road where your perspective becomes wider as you walk down it. As you react to the larger world through this particular self, you expand that self and in a sense this expands your awareness. You become more aware of what the world is like, but this happens only within the boundaries defined by this self. The farther you walk away from the center, the more you expand your perspective so it seems like a good thing to walk away from the center—and this is indeed what you are meant to do. You are meant to expand your awareness of the world as an intermediate step towards expanding your self-awareness.

One day you reach the circumference of the circle, and now you simply cannot expand your perspective on the world any more through this particular self. How do you grow in consciousness from this level? If you have not entered separation, you still know that you are a point-like self in the center of the circle. You can therefore easily turn around and look towards the center, you can instantly abandon the self you have created (letting it die or giving up this life in order to return to the center). You do this by saying: "I have not become this self, I am more than this self." Once back in the center, you can choose another self and repeat the process. Once you have gone around the

circle and experienced life in the material world from
all 360 angles (in reality many more are possible), you
can come to the conclusion: "I am more than any self
in this world," meaning you are ready to enter the process of ascending to a higher world. Your causal body
will contain the experiences of seeing the world from
all these different perspectives and you will have many
nuances in your causal body.

Return to free will

What we can now gain from this illustration is that when a
lifestream is new, it has only a limited self-awareness. You are
still standing in the center of a circle, but your initial circle is
very small and it does not have 360 degrees. It may only have
two so what you see is that you can choose to go in one of
two directions. We might say that instead of standing in a circle, you see yourself as standing on a road, and you can go in
either one direction or the other. As you do make a choice and
experience the consequences of that choice, you expand your
awareness of the world, which also expands your self-awareness. The more experiences you get, the more you expand your
vision and the more options you can see. The greater your circle, the more degrees it can contain and the more options you
have to choose from.

We now see that when we talk about free will, we have two
considerations. To give you another visual illustration, imagine
you are standing in a circular room. The room has a number
of doors. Obviously, the number of doors that the room can
have depends on the size of the room. The greater the circumference of the circle, the more doors, meaning you have more
options to choose from. At any given time, the circle of your
self-awareness has a certain circumference, meaning you can

choose from a certain amount of options. Let us say your present room has 12 doors. We can now say that ideally this means you have complete freedom to choose which one of the 12 doors you will walk through. Nothing restricts which door you choose, but, of course, your choice is not entirely free. You can only choose from the doors you can see, and thus the circumference of your self-awareness does indeed limit your free will.

Now we will give this a twist by saying that your room still has 12 doors, but some of them have been blocked from your view by screens set up in the room. Other doors have been painted red, and you have come to believe that a red door is dangerous. This illustrates how the fallen beings are seeking to restrict your free will. They will seek to prevent you from seeing certain options and they will seek to make you believe that other options are somehow dangerous and should not be chosen. They would like you to believe you have only two options, namely to either accept their world view or to oppose it. They want you to believe that their world view is of God and that anything else is of the devil. They are the blind leaders who want you to follow them blindly.

Freedom of will and rebellion

One of the more subtle ideas floated by the fallen beings is that human beings were originally created as a kind of robots who could only obey the will of an external god. The only way to gain true freedom of will is to rebel against this tyrannical god, decide that he doesn't exist and therefore accept that you are fully capable of defining what constitutes right and wrong choices. It is even said by some that the devil was the first being who claimed his free will by rebelling against the tyrannical god in the sky. We can now see why these ideas are out of touch with reality.

There is no tyrannical god in the sky. The concept of a remote god that has a specific form is entirely the creation of the fallen beings. Only a god who has form can have a will that it wants to impose upon you because only a god that has form could be threatened by anything you might do. If this god wasn't threatened, how could it be concerned about what you do in the world of form?

You were not created to follow the will of any external authority. You were created with a point-like self that can go in any direction. The only thing that limits your options is the size of the circle of your self-awareness. As long as you freely choose among the options you can see, you will gain experience and expand your circle of awareness, thereby expanding your options. The Creator wants you to choose freely among your options and thereby expand your options, continuing to do so until you reach the Creator consciousness.

What is really behind this claim? The fallen beings want to be as the tyrannical god they have created. In defining this all-powerful god, they have defined the kind of power they want here on earth. They seek to get that power by getting all people to follow them blindly. They are the ones who want to control your will, and they even project that you will gain freedom only by submitting to them.

What does it mean to make truly free choices? Two conditions must be fulfilled:

• You have a clear and unrestricted vision of all options available to you.

• You have full understanding of the consequences of each option.

How do you fulfill these conditions? Ultimately, only by attaining the Christ consciousness. The central concern about free will is this: Will a choice you make right now limit the choices you can make in the future?

Ponder this carefully. The reality is that God has given you a will that is entirely free and only dependent on your self-awareness. Because your will is free, you can exercise it in two ways:

•   You can make choices that expand your sense of self. This means that any choice you make will help you see more options and give you more choices in the future.

•   You can make choices that limit your sense of self. This means any choice will decrease the options you can see and give you less options in the future.

Attaining the Christ consciousness means that you realize you are a spiritual being. This means you are a formless being who cannot be limited by any form in the material world. In order to act within the world of form, you have created a form-based self. You can at any time chose to transcend your current sense of self. What the fallen beings want you to believe is that you can make certain choices that can never be undone. You can use your free will to make a choice that takes away your free will. Once you have made that choice, you are trapped forever, unless you follow the only way out as the fallen beings have defined it.

What have I said about the Conscious You? In reality it is who it is. You can choose to step into a certain self and see the world through it, and this will indeed help you expand your self-awareness. You can even choose to step into a separate self and thereby forget that you are a formless being. Regardless of how you see yourself right now, you have not become that self. You are still the point-like being that descended and you can at any time return to your center and thereby step outside any self created in this world.

This is the reality given to you by the formless God and taught by its representatives, the ascended masters. The fallen beings want to get you to step into a self they have created and then they want you to believe you can never step out of it. The epic dramas are the weapon they use to trap you in a form-based self.

Did God make a mistake? No, the fallen beings made a mistake by rebelling against God's design. They could do this because they have free will. They claim God made a mistake by giving beings free will, but they will not give up their own free will. They want you to give up your free will and follow them blindly. How long will you let this continue? When will you reclaim your freedom of will, decide to walk away from your limited self and follow the Living Christ into an unlimited self?

12 | A SPECIFIC OUTCOME MUST BE ACHIEVED

Another subtle consequence of the epic world view is that it projects the idea that on earth a specific outcome must be achieved in order to manifest God's plan and avoid the worst possible disaster. This is a very serpentine idea that has trapped numerous spiritual people in various blind alleys so I will look at it from different angles.

Any experience can help you grow

I have said that you have free will and you have the right to have any experience possible on earth until you have had enough of it and want something higher. What determines the kind of experience you desire to have? Naturally, you cannot desire to have an experience that you cannot see as a possibility. Before the fallen beings arrived on this planet, many of the experiences that people today take for granted simply were not available. Large scale conflict, what you today call war, had not taken place on this planet so having the experience of being a warrior or a general commanding vast armies was simply not in the field of view of human beings. They couldn't even desire it because they couldn't see it as a possibility.

This is where certain fallen beings would take what I said earlier and say that this proves people were restricted in how they exercised their free will. The fallen beings have given people greater freedom of will by showing them options they could not see on their own. From a certain perspective, I would even say this is correct. Why did the karmic board allow fallen beings to embody on earth? Because the inhabitants of earth had already gone into the struggle consciousness. By allowing the fallen beings to embody here, the struggle would be intensified and this would have the effect that people would more quickly have had enough of the struggle.

From an overall perspective, any experience that is possible in the material universe can serve to take you to the point where you have had enough of that kind of experience and want something higher. Any experience you can have through separation can serve to take you to the point where you have had enough of the struggle and want more, therefore reaching for the Christ consciousness.

What we need to add here is that what the fallen beings did was to help people see options that would limit their self-awareness even more than what human beings had envisioned themselves. The fallen beings did not actually free people. They deceived them into limiting their self-awareness whereby they blindly follow the fallen beings. As I have said, this can also expand your self-awareness but only when you awaken from the illusion.

What we now see is that in the original scenario, lifestreams would be on a path that would gradually expand their self-awareness. It was a steady upward curve where people never took a backward step. After the fallen beings arrived here, most people have gone into a downward spiral of limiting their self-awareness. The downward momentum continued until people had created such an intense struggle for themselves that they could no longer stand it and cried out for deliverance.

People have then gone through a very abrupt awakening, have asked for our help and we have given it in order to help them climb to a higher level of self-awareness. Some have then been ensnared by another serpentine illusion and have again started limiting their self-awareness. Again, they had to hit bottom before they asked for help and again we delivered it.

From a purely pragmatic perspective, this process can eventually lead people to have seen so much struggle that they give up the entire struggle consciousness. This will also lead to a growth in self-awareness, but it will include infinitely more suffering than the steady upward progress designed by the ascended masters. Beyond the suffering, there is also a mechanism that makes the epic dramas a very serious trap that can delay the awakening for many people.

The cost of making choices

In the original scenario, people would make choices, observe the consequences and then use their experience to make new choices. In this scenario, it never even entered their minds to consider that they might have made a wrong choice. Why would they think so when every choice led to consequences that caused them to expand their self-awareness and experience life as richer than before?

With the advent of the fallen beings and their epic dramas, a new consideration was projected into the collective consciousness, namely that certain choices are right and certain choices are wrong. How was this achieved? By defining that there is a specific outcome here on earth that must come to pass according to God's plan. This led to a very subtle shift in people's approach to life. Before, people had the approach that the goal of life was the growth in self-awareness. Any choice you make leads to consequences and you learn from the consequences by evaluating: "Do I want more of this or do I want less of this?" The overall result is that you learn from all choices and that you expand your self-awareness. You know what works for you and what doesn't work for you, which means you also learn who you are. We might say that people's focus was on producing a result that reaches beyond the material world, namely growth in self-awareness.

In the fallen scenario the focus of life suddenly became to produce specific results here in the material world. It was projected that producing this material result was more important than your individual growth in self-awareness. You should submit your individual will and growth to bringing about this collective result. There was now a new way to evaluate the consequences of your choices. It was no longer about what leads to growth, it was a matter of what was right and wrong based on the superior standard (a standard defined by the fallen beings).

The arrival of the fallen beings happened a long time ago, so long ago that it can't easily be fitted into the current understanding of human history. For a very long time, countless people have fed their energy and attention into creating a spirit in the collective consciousness. This spirit, or beast, has become very powerful and there is now such a force directed at people that most people simply cannot see what is right and wrong about right and wrong. They uncritically accept that there is an overall standard for what is right and what is wrong and that such a standard was defined by God. They unknowingly submit to the beast and become blind followers of the fallen leaders. In order to rise above a certain level of Christhood, you have to come to see the fallacy of this entire mindset so let me give you a teaching on this.

All human beings have been affected by this spirit that there *must* be a standard for right and wrong. Many spiritual seekers have transferred that to their spiritual teaching and even our students believe the ascended masters have defined a standard for what is right and wrong. What is the most subtle psychological effect of this mindset? It is that if you make certain choices, those choices were wrong. Because of the intense momentum created over eons of time, it is very difficult to admit a mistake because most people cannot stop themselves from going into deep feelings of guilt, self-blame, fear and other negative emotions.

The subtle psychological consequence is that before the advent of the fallen beings, it was very easy for people to change their choices. If a choice produced a consequence they did not want more of, they simply made a different choice, abandoning the old one. They didn't think: "Oh, I made a mistake, I was wrong and that makes me a bad person." They simply changed their minds and moved on.

Today, admitting that one of your choices was not the best one carries a major penalty. You made a mistake that can be wrong in an epic sense with all of the negative emotions that might produce. What is the effect? That it has now become very tempting to avoid admitting that you "were wrong," making it much more difficult for you to change direction in life. Once you have gone into the epic mindset, it becomes very difficult to get back out.

The catch-22 of wrong choices

The epic mindset defines that certain choices are wrong in an epic way. When you go into duality, you automatically enter a struggle against other people, and this will lead you to take actions that have epic consequences. Sooner or later the struggle will make you feel so overwhelmed by negative feelings that you kill another human being in anger. Killing another human being is an epic act, and for most people it will lead to the inner realization that they have done something wrong. This will cause them to open themselves up to the emotional spirit that projects guilt and blame at them, and the result can be such an overwhelming negative feeling that they simply cannot live with it. In their extreme agony and pain, they look for a way out.

Why did you kill the other person in the first place? In many cases, this happened because people were relentlessly attacked and violated by the aggressive fallen beings. One group of fallen beings caused people to start killing in self-defense. The other group projected that killing is wrong, but they also offered people a way out of the guilt. Because when there is an epic goal that *must* be attained, then any act which accomplishes this goal becomes justifiable.

This now leads to a consideration that new co-creators could never have come up with on their own, namely that the end can justify the means. As I said, human beings have a sense of kinship with each other and a basic reverence for life. The fallen beings have neither, and they will kill anyone standing in their way without feeling remorse over doing so. The fallen beings forced people to go into the struggle and start killing. They then offered people a way to avoid the sense of guilt, the price being that people had to accept the epic mindset. Yes, killing is wrong, but these other people are killing our people in order to destroy God's plan, which means it is justified for us to kill them in order to manifest the outcome God wants. We will even be rewarded for this in heaven. This can now suck people into a spiral of being a warrior who is seemingly always fighting on the side of good, meaning that over several lifetimes people can kill many others in war and they can themselves be killed many times. I trust you can see that killing others leads you to create karma, no matter how justified it might seem according to the standard defined by the fallen beings. I trust you can also see that participating in armed conflict and being killed will lead to trauma that creates deep scars in your psychology and misqualifies enormous amounts of energy. This brings me to the catch-22 and the question of how people might escape from this downward spiral of struggle and killing.

The essence of the epic mindset is that you can make choices that are wrong in an ultimate way. Doing this would lead to maximum emotional pain. With this in mind, what is the worst possible choice you could ever make? It would be to go into the duality consciousness and become a blind follower of the fallen beings.

How could you ever escape this state? You would have to consciously admit that your choice was not one you wish to continue. The problem is that when people begin to see that the actions they have taken through the duality consciousness were not the best ones, they are still colored by the duality consciousness. This causes them to evaluate all choices based on right and wrong, meaning that if it was a mistake to go into duality, then you did something wrong and that makes you a bad person. You are then overwhelmed by intense negative feelings.

This exposes the basic strategy of the fallen beings. They trick you into going into duality and enter the struggle against others. They trick you into doing things that make karma for yourself. As you have had enough of the struggle and killing and want to get out, they then project at you that if you admit how wrong you have been, it will be so painful that it will destroy you. They seek to keep you endlessly in the mindset of affirming the epic world view where your actions were justifiable according to some ultimate cause. They want you to believe that in a short while, good will win the ultimate victory over evil—if only you keep believing that killing is justified.

How will you ever break free of the fallen mindset? Only by consciously seeing and admitting that you no longer want to be in this frame of mind. If you cannot consciously admit this because of the pain it would cause you, then it is very tempting to take another round in the epic mindset where your actions feel justified and you can avoid the pain and the "day of reckoning."

What is the only possible way out? It is, as I have explained earlier, to acknowledge that the Conscious You is responsible for entering the separate self, but it is not responsible for the actions committed by the separate self. The fallen beings have attempted to block even this way out.

Does God condemn you?

It is implicit in the epic dramas that God has defined the outcome that he wants to see manifest on earth. God has therefore also defined the standard for right and wrong actions, meaning that God himself will condemn you for doing wrong actions. How can you accept what I just said above as long as you hold on to the fallen image of the angry and judgmental god in the sky? The simple fact is that you can't, which means you must deny what I said and take another round in the epic mindset.

Does the real God condemn you? The Creator doesn't even see anything you do in duality. As the Bible says, his eyes cannot behold iniquity. The Creator has given you the right to go into duality, but once you do, God does not see anything you do there. We of the ascended masters do see what you do in duality, but we do not condemn you for it. We know you are acting through a separate self. We know that the Conscious You can at any time see the unreality of this separate self and decide to step outside of it. As I have said, as long as you are not open to escaping the separate self, we are not concerned about what you do because you will learn from the School of Hard Knocks. When you become open to escaping, we step in to help you. Our only concern is to get you to let go of the old sense of self and accept a self that is closer to oneness, closer to Christ consciousness. Once you truly let go of an old self and the consciousness it was created from, you are "blameless before God." You have been reborn into a new self that does not even remember what the old self did. As the Bible says: "I will remember their sins no more."

We have no blame towards anyone and only seek to help all transcend the limited self. Due to the mechanics of the situation, you can escape a given self only by consciously coming to see its limitations and then choosing to leave them behind. We never blame you, but until you have fully let go of the fallen consciousness, you will often blame yourself. For many people this causes them to go into a twilight zone where they are asking for our help, but at the same time they are seeking to hide from us so that we do not see their imperfection.

I have explained that what caused you to lose contact with your spiritual teacher was that you sought to hide from the teacher. As long as you are seeking to hide from us, we cannot help you fully. Why? Because we cannot help you fully see the limitations of your present sense of self, which means you cannot separate yourself from it.

We are not directing blame upon you. You are projecting upon us that we blame you, and you are then seeking to hide certain things from us in order to avoid the blame that you think we have for those actions. This is all a projection of your own mind. If you could come to see this, you would make it so much easier for us to help you and so much easier for yourself to rise to a new level of freedom where the prince of this world no longer has anything in you. It is a basic fact that you cannot take full advantage of a true teacher as long as you seek to hide something from that teacher. It is what you are not willing to look at that keeps you imprisoned in the old self and the fallen consciousness. There is nothing hidden that shall not be revealed.

What about the golden age?

At this point, some will ask that if the ascended masters don't have a specific outcome we want to see manifest on earth, why do we keep talking about a golden age? Let us first consider the outcome that the fallen beings want to see manifest. What they are projecting into the collective consciousness is that there is a fixed and unchangeable image of a perfect society, and this is what God wants to see manifest. Once this state has been achieved, the earth has become perfect and it will remain in this state forever.

In reality, the most experienced fallen beings have begun to understand that in an unascended sphere nothing can ever stand still. They have, in previous spheres, pursued the dream of creating a society in which they were the undisputed leaders whose power and privileges could never be threatened. They have often come close to creating such a society, but every time the second law of thermodynamics snatched the victory from their grasp. In reality, which hardly any of the fallen beings have grasped, it is precisely the fallen beings themselves who destroy their own perfect society. The Karmic Board is not stupid so they never allow one fallen being to embody on a planet. There is always at least two fallen beings with the same level of attainment, meaning they will both want ultimate power and end up in a rivalry against each other. This ensures that one fallen being cannot gain ultimate power, at least not for long. There will always be an aspiring power elite seeking to overthrow the established power elite.

There are, however, some fallen beings who have realized that a static society will never be possible so they are not truly seeking it. They are only projecting that this is the goal because it fools most people on earth. As long as you are blinded by separation, a stable society will seem like a perfectly desirable and attainable goal. It is only when you have a direct experience of infinity that you realize nothing can or should stand still in the material world, as it would defeat the purpose of constant growth towards an infinite sense of self.

The most experienced fallen beings are not truly seeking a fixed society. They are seeking to maintain the struggle because they know that the dream of a perfect society is the best motivation for getting people to fight an enemy that seemingly opposes the dream. They are simply lying to people in order to keep them in the struggle and they know the goal can never be fulfilled.

The ascended masters also know that in the world of form, and especially in an unascended sphere, no static society could be achieved. Saint Germain does have a vision of what could be achieved in the Aquarian age, but it is not a fixed vision of a static society. Our goal is to create a society that gives its members the maximum opportunity to raise their level of self-awareness. As some people take advantage of this and raise their consciousness, society naturally needs to change so that these people can rise even higher.

A golden age society will be constantly transcending itself, as you have indeed seen many societies on earth change over the past century. The rate of change you see today is slow compared to what it will be in the golden age. When The Golden Age of Saint Germain becomes more manifest, society will change so rapidly that people will be raised to the ascension point much more quickly than today. When you step outside the fallen consciousness, you see as self-evident that the ascended masters do not have a fixed vision that we want to see manifest on earth. Our vision is a society that is giving its members the maximum opportunity for raising their consciousness. This means that it is never justified to use violence or force in order to manifest the golden age society. Saint Germain has given profound teachings [See *www.ascendedmasterlight.com*] on the fact that in the golden age an entirely new kind of technology will be released, namely a form of technology that is not based on force. He has also said that before this can happen, a critical mass of people must have risen beyond the force-based mindset of the fallen beings.

Saint Germain is waiting for his best students to achieve this goal, and one purpose for me giving these ego discourses is to help people rise above the force-based mindset and the serpentine illusion that the ends can justify the means. How long will Saint Germain have to wait for *you*?

What about my divine plan?

We have given teachings that before you come into embodiment you meet with your ascended teachers in order to formulate a plan for your next lifetime. This might specify certain things you want to accomplish during that lifetime so it would seem as if there is a goal to accomplish something in the material world. It might even specify certain things you have to do so how is this different from the epic dramas? Couldn't it be part of your divine plan that you accomplish something to bring Saint Germain's Golden Age into manifestation? Again, the epic scenario projected by the fallen beings is not real. The goal they define is not the same as the goal for the golden age defined by Saint Germain. The crucial difference is that for an ascended master, the ends cannot justify the means, meaning we do not advocate the use of force or violence in order to accomplish a certain material goal. Of course, there are certain material goals that are part of Saint Germain's plan for the golden age. If it is in your divine plan to help bring a certain goal into manifestation, you should indeed dedicate your life to its fulfillment.

Many spiritual people do indeed have the goal to accomplish a particular task on earth. There is nothing wrong with this, as long as you do not use force and as long as you do not become attached to the outcome. What the fallen beings have done is to take advantage of your rightful longing to help bring society forward. They seek to redirect it into the epic dramas whereby you actually do not help bring society forward.

The difference is subtle. You may look at one person who accomplishes a particular goal, say bringing forth the invention of a new piece of technology. Yet the person has an impure motive and is willing to use force to get his invention developed and produced. You may then look at another person who also has the creativity of bringing forth something new but is not willing to use force and thus is not successful. Which one helped bring society forward?

The first one did manifest a physical result, but in doing so he also perpetuated the dualistic struggle. The other one did not manifest a result but did not perpetuate the struggle and did indeed free himself from the consciousness of the struggle. Look at my mission 2,000 years ago. Right after my death on the cross it would seem as if I had accomplished nothing and had left no physical result behind. From a spiritual perspective my mission was a success because I qualified for my ascension, brought new ideas into the physical and I brought the judgment of those who killed me. In many cases you can fulfill your divine plan without having the physical result because that result can always be brought forth by someone else. As you get closer to your ascension, physical results become less and less important.

Take note that I gave some very radical directions: Resist not evil, turn the other cheek, forgive seventy times seven, let the dead bury their dead. These are directions for those who are close to their ascension and who want to make maximum progress towards that non-material goal. In that case, you need to demonstrate that you are free of the epic struggle, even to the point where you will not kill someone who attempts to kill you.

One of the things you have to do in order to qualify for your ascension is to balance karma. If you have made karma by engaging in the epic struggle, how can you balance that karma? Not by engaging the struggle in this lifetime. For people who are not close to their ascension, it can be appropriate to defend themselves, but for those close to the ascension this might be detrimental to their progress. You cannot be so attached to a physical result, including your physical survival, that you are willing to use force and thereby perpetuate the force-based struggle.

In order to qualify for your ascension you have to come to a point where there is nothing you have to do on this planet and there is nothing you want to do or experience. There are indeed people in embodiment right now who could qualify for their ascensions in this lifetime. The only thing keeping them from accomplishing this goal is that they have not let go of the epic mindset. They feel they cannot leave this planet behind until the goal – as defined by their spiritual teaching – of defeating the enemy has been accomplished. Some of these people have completely closed their minds to the ascended masters because they use an epic illusion to refute our words.

Stop making choices

Let us look at another subtle effect of the concept that there are right and wrong choices. As I have said, in the original scenario, there was no risk associated with making choices. You simply learned from all choices and expanded your sense of self. With the advent of the fallen beings and their standard for right and wrong choices, there is a severe emotional risk associated with making wrong choices. You can be wrong in an epic way and have to suffer the worst possible consequences, such as eternal suffering in hell.

In a sense, it is true that your choices can lead to suffering. Yet the choices that lead to suffering are the choices made from the consciousness of duality. The choices that could bring you to the extreme suffering of a hellish state of mind are the choices made from the epic consciousness of the fallen beings.

Once again, you see that the fallen beings have created the problem and they now seek to offer you a solution. The solution is that you use your free will to decide that you are such an incompetent being that you could not possibly decide what constitutes right and wrong choices. You will give up making your own choices and follow a standard defined by those who claim they have the right and the wisdom to define this standard. You will give up making your own choices and blindly do what the fallen beings tell you to do—for surely, then you could never make wrong choices.

There are two things wrong with this scenario. As I have already explained, the safety mechanism of the cosmic mirror will return to you what you send out. When you base your choices on the standard of the fallen beings, suffering will inevitably follow. What the fallen beings will do is to offer you another epic drama that can explain away your suffering. It is not because you are blindly following the fallen beings, it is because something outside yourself is making you suffer. The solution is to once again submit to a drama and start fighting the cause of your suffering. The other problem with the scenario is that it is contrary to the purpose of creation, which is your growth in self-awareness. You do not grow by blindly doing what other beings tell you to do. You grow by making your own choices and then consciously learning from the consequences. The epic dramas make it seem unnecessary to evaluate the consequences, as they always have an explanation that places the responsibility away from yourself.

Finally, consider how you might escape the treadmill of blindly following the blind leaders. You got on that treadmill by deciding that you would not make your own choices. How can you get off again? Only by deciding to take back your power to make your own choices. The epic dramas tell you that this is the worst thing you could possibly do because it would surely cause you to be condemned to hell. In reality, it is blindly following the fallen beings that might take you to hell. The *only* possible "salvation" is to start making your own choices and ask for the guidance from the Christ consciousness.

You now see that the fallen beings first create a problem, and then they present you with an escape mechanism. When it turns out that this escape is not really an escape from suffering, they seek to block you from doing the only thing that could truly help you escape from the treadmill of the duality consciousness. How long will you let this continue? I stand ready to help you at any time, but you must decide to open your mind to the truth that will set you free. Seek and ye shall find, ask and ye shall receive, knock and the door shall be opened for you.

13 | DO YOU KNOW BETTER THAN GOD?

As I have just explained, the only way out of suffering is to start to make your own choices and ask for guidance from the Christ mind. It should be no surprise that the fallen beings have attempted to block this way out. A very dangerous effect of the epic mindset is that it makes people think they know better than God or the ascended masters. They use a specific teaching or idea that is in the physical realm as a justification for refusing either our teachings given as progressive revelation or the words and ideas we give them directly within their own minds. You would scarcely believe how many people who actually know about ascended masters but have rejected valid directions they get from within themselves, either from their Christ selves, their I AM Presences or from their personal ascended teachers. This is clearly the greatest single obstacle for our efforts to free individuals and raise the collective consciousness.

A special concern in this respect is that there are many people who have come to accept a specific outer teaching as coming from us and therefore being a valid teaching. They now use the outer teaching that is in the physical as a justification for rejecting the Living Word that we seek to give them from within. There are even those who are still so absolutely convinced about the validity of the epic dramas that they have interpreted ascended master teachings from the epic mindset, being convinced that we really do affirm the epic struggle and the necessity to defeat dark forces.

These people will take our teachings about fallen beings and reason that it is justified to use force or violence in order to remove the fallen beings from the earth and defeat their schemes. Look back at history and see how much warring has taken place on this planet. If it had been possible to remove the fallen beings through violence, don't you think it would have already happened?

By the very fact that it has not happened, it should be obvious that it is not possible to remove the fallen beings through violence. The simple reason is that every act of violence perpetuates the epic struggle and thus helps the fallen beings stay in embodiment and stay in control. The fallen beings were allowed to come to this planet because a critical mass of human beings had gone into duality. They will be removed only when a critical mass of human beings transcend duality. It would be a joy for us if those who claim to be our students would be among the first to take this step into a new state of consciousness where you are wise to the serpents but so harmless that they cannot pull you into the struggle. Of course, what I have said here is not obvious to those still blinded by duality. They will insist that the epic struggle is real and they will even quote our previous teachings in order to prove their point.

The reality of progressive revelation

What I am doing through this messenger is progressive revelation. In the past, we have brought forth teachings through other messengers that were also examples of valid progressive revelation. What does it mean that revelation is progressive? In the 1930s we brought forth certain teachings that were specifically designed to help people at a certain level of consciousness transcend that level. As I have said before, we had to give these teachings in such a way that the people at this level could accept them, meaning they would have to contain elements that were defined by the limitations of people's consciousness. The teachings also contained elements that could help people go beyond that level.

As a critical mass of people used these teachings to rise to a higher level, it became possible for us to bring forth new teachings designed for a higher level of consciousness. These teachings did not contain some of the limiting elements from the previous teaching, and this caused some students of the earlier teachings to reject them because they did not validate some of their cherished beliefs. They also contained elements that went beyond the old teaching and this caused other students to reject them because they seemingly contradicted previous teachings.

Some students did take the new teachings and they used them to transcend the level of consciousness for which the teachings were designed. This once again gave us the authorization to bring forth teachings for the next level of consciousness. When will this process stop? When the last person has ascended from earth—and realistically, that is quite a ways into the future.

There are, of course, still many people in embodiment who have not transcended the level of consciousness addressed in the teachings we gave in the 1930s or even earlier. There is nothing wrong with people focusing on the teaching suited to their level of consciousness and ignoring later teachings. Yet any ascended master student should be very careful to avoid using one teaching to reject a later teaching. If your use of a given teaching is successful, it is only natural that you transcend a certain level of consciousness. Once you have done so, you will not have maximum growth by continuing to follow that teaching for the rest of this lifetime. You will only have maximum growth by stepping up to the next teaching and continuing to do so as you get inner direction. Of course, if you fix your outer mind on having to follow a specific outer teaching for the rest of your life, you will reject that inner direction, won't you?

Many ascended master students have the potential to truly overcome the epic mindset in this lifetime. In order to do so, they have to be willing to look at the fact that the epic mindset makes people's egos think they know better than God and better than the ascended masters. It is essential for your growth that you make an effort to step outside your outer self and experience the pure awareness that is the open door to direct contact with your I AM Presence and your ascended teachers. Only then will you be able to accept the direction that we offer you directly within yourself. Take note that I am not telling you to follow an outer teaching, not even this messenger and teaching. I am telling you to follow your inner direction—once you are able to receive it. We have given many tools for helping you open your mind to that inner direction. [See *www.transcendencetoolbox.com*.]

Did God lie to Adam and Eve?

The fallen beings will do anything they can think of to deceive human beings into following them. In every time period they have attempted to set themselves up as leaders of society, even religious leaders. They have often been there at crucial moments in world history, and they have managed to exert their influence and take humanity in a less than ideal direction, a direction that perpetuated the dualistic struggle. This includes being able to pervert many religious scriptures.

The account in Genesis of the fall of Adam of Eve is in subtle ways perverted by the fallen beings. It is stated that God had told Adam and Eve that they were allowed to eat of all of the fruits in the garden except the fruit of the knowledge of good and evil. If they did eat of this forbidden fruit, they would surely die. This is not correct.

The students in Maitreya's Mystery School had been told that the Tree of the Knowledge of Good and Evil was a specific state of consciousness, namely the consciousness of duality. They had been told that it was an initiation that they would have to take but only when the teacher assessed that they were ready for it. They had been told that if they took the initiation too early, they would most likely become trapped in duality, meaning they would lose contact with the teacher and be trapped in separation. They had been told that in that case, they could not remain in the Mystery School and the teacher could not help them as they would not be able to hear his instructions. They had even been told that by going into separation, their old sense of self, as a being connected to the teacher, would die and they would be reborn into a new, separate self.

In a sense, one could say that it was correct that they would die if they ate the forbidden fruit. One can also say that the serpent was correct in that they would not die. What can resolve the paradox? Self-awareness has two components: "self" and "awareness." Self is temporary but awareness is ongoing. At any given time, you see yourself as and through a specific self, meaning your awareness is experiencing itself through the filter of that self. The self can be replaced by another self, and when this happens the former self dies. Because of the ongoing nature of awareness, you may not be conscious of this shift.

You simply experience life through the new self without realizing that the old self has died and you have taken on another one.

A new co-creator starts with a point-like sense of self. For quite some time, the circle of self will be so small that a co-creator will not be consciously aware that it shifts into a new self and that the old one dies. It is not even conscious of the difference between how the old and the new self looks at life. Only when you reach a certain level of maturity will you be able to be conscious of the shift and retain an awareness of the difference between old and new. Only then will you be able to go into duality without losing the awareness that you are not a separate self but that there is more to your existence.

Experienced students can experiment with duality like an actor who takes on a costume and plays Hamlet. The actor may be fully living himself into the role, temporarily forgetting everything else. Yet there comes a point where he again remembers that he has not become Hamlet, he is only playing a role, meaning he can take off the costume and leave the theater. If you do not have sufficient self-awareness, then you cannot experiment with duality without losing yourself in the role. You will surely die as the old self and be reborn as a new separate self. This is what has happened to all human beings in embodiment on earth. It has happened because of the deception of the fallen beings.

Serpentine logic

How did the fallen beings deceive human beings? They used some form of serpentine logic to get them to step into a specific state of consciousness. This state of consciousness is very difficult to see once you are inside of it so I caution you to use your intuitive abilities and not the analytical mind to follow what I am saying. Before a being falls, it sees itself as a self that is connected to something greater than itself. It knows that it is not complete in and of itself but that it is an extension of something greater. This is the I AM Presence, although a new co-creator has no conscious awareness of the Presence, only a sense of being connected to something. The being knows that it is not capable of knowing reality on its own, it needs a frame of reference from outside itself. That is why the student is connected to the teacher and listens to the teacher. The obvious advantage is that you are never alone and you never have to face an initiation or problem on your own. You always have access to your spiritual teacher, and although he or she will not tell you what to do, the teacher will give you a frame of reference that is invaluable.

As Maitreya explains in greater depth, there comes a point when the student has to start becoming self-sufficient. The teacher must withdraw and allow the student to make decisions on its own. The student will still be connected to the teacher and will make a decision, then go back to the teacher to get feedback about the lesson that can be learned. The teacher therefore serves as the student's frame of reference and it is the teacher's directions that form the basis for how the student evaluates its decisions and their outcome. This prevents the mind of the student from becoming a closed system.

The consciousness of duality represents the opposite of this frame of mind. The dualistic mind is indeed a closed system, meaning it has no frame of reference from outside the material universe. As an individual you may have a frame of reference from outside your mind, but that frame will not be a spiritual teacher. It will be something coming from the material world, meaning it will be a thought system devised by the fallen beings. The fallen beings have become your frame of reference, meaning that all decisions you make and all evaluations you perform will keep you trapped in the dualistic struggle. When you are in duality, you make decisions based on your current frame of mind (as you do before entering duality), but you also evaluate the outcome of your decisions based on your current frame of mind.

You are literally defining your own standard for evaluating your decisions, which means it is possible to define a standard so it seems like your decisions are always right or necessary. As the serpent said, you have become as a god defining good and evil. The net effect is that you do not need to learn from your decisions, meaning that a decision does not expand your self-awareness. Instead, it solidifies your current self and makes you think you need to hold on to it instead of rising to a higher one.

If you know something about science, you will know that it has been proven mathematically that in reality there are no self-referential systems [Gödel's Theorem]. A closed system will contain internal contradictions that cannot be resolved from within the system itself. There is always a need to look beyond any system that can be created in this world. This is also described in the second law of thermodynamics, which says that any closed system will self-destruct. This is the absolute reality about the consciousness of duality and any system or effort based upon it here on earth. This is also the reality that the fallen beings will deny as long as they remain trapped in the fallen consciousness. They will do anything to make you deny this reality as well, and their greatest ally is your personal ego. Its survival depends on you denying this reality.

The ego is always right

I have talked about the ego's need for security and I have said that the ego can always come up with an argument that makes it seem right. This is easy to understand when you compare it to my illustration about the Conscious You standing in the center of a circle with 360 degrees, each forming a triangular, pie-shaped area. Each slice of the pie represents one way to experience life on earth.

You are meant to go into one slice and experience life through it until you reach the circumference of the circle and have had enough of experiencing life this way. As long as you are a connected being, you will then return to center, pick another slice and experience life that way. As you go around the circle and experience life from many different angles, you gradually expand your self-awareness until you realize that you are more than any self that could be built on earth. You then begin to long for a higher experience than what is possible on earth and you enter the ascension process.

What also happens as you do this is that you realize something very profound. You are a formless being and you can never be defined by or trapped in any self on earth. As you experience life through many different selves, you come to realize that there is no final or ultimate self. There are many ways to experience life on earth and none of them are better or "right" in some epic sense. They are simply different experiences and none of them have any enduring reality or value. They are temporary tools for expanding your self-awareness and the last thing you want is to get stuck in any one of them.

As a practical example, you realize that the real purpose of a religious teaching is (or should be if the fallen beings had not perverted it) to help you raise your consciousness. There can be many valid religious teachings that can all help people raise their consciousness. It is meaningless to try to establish one as the superior or only true one, and it is especially meaningless to enter the epic mindset of seeking to forcefully eradicate all other religions. You clearly see religion as a tool, as something you need to transcend. You also begin to realize that it is meaningless to say that any religious teaching could represent a superior or infallible truth. Words and images from the material world simply cannot capture the ineffable reality of the spiritual realm, a reality that the Conscious You is beginning to experience directly. Nothing from this world could ever be an infallible truth, and in order to know reality, you need to experience the Spirit of Truth, which the Conscious You is capable of doing. The only condition being that you become so non-attached to your current self that you will allow the Conscious You to step outside that self.

What the fallen beings have managed to do is to get people to step into one slice of the pie and then think this is the only right way to experience life. They are then automatically threatened by all of the other people who experience life on earth through a different slice. When you add the epic mindset, it seems as if God has defined your slice as the only one and God wants you to eradicate all the other slices—or the world will come to an end.

How is this attained? It is attained by saying that life can only be seen as it appears when seen through your particular slice. Any other perspective is wrong and of the devil and you need to automatically reject it. When you reject enough contrary evidence, you can always prove your point and it always seems as if the ego is right.

Diversity is the way to help the Conscious You expand its sense of self and avoid becoming stuck in a particular self. The fallen beings have managed to make people think diversity is dangerous and will lead to the death of your self. This is, of course, correct. As you have gone to the outer limits of your current self and return to center, your current self will die. The Conscious You will not die but will seamlessly move into another self. In the beginning you will not be conscious of this, but as you experience sufficient diversity, you will become conscious of the fact that your earth-based self can die without you dying.

The fallen beings have managed to pervert the very process that is meant to take you toward greater self-awareness and the ascension. Instead, they have trapped you in an ongoing quest to take one unreal and temporary self and use it to destroy other selves. They have projected the subtle idea that when you are successful, the self that has conquered all others will become permanent and God will let it into his kingdom. A completely futile quest that will never come to fruition, as my parable about the wedding feast illustrates. You will never enter the kingdom by raising one self to some ultimate status on earth. You will enter only by coming to realize that you are more than any self on earth whereby you put on the wedding garment of the Christ consciousness.

The choice is simple. Will you continue the process of seeking to prove yourself right according to a standard defined by the fallen beings? Or will you reach for the mind of Christ than can help you rise above all standards defined on earth? Will you continue to seek to prove yourself right among men, or will you choose to be right with God? You cannot do both, you cannot serve God and mammon.

If the Conscious You
identifies itself
fully with the drama,
your mind will be closed
to anything that a spiritual teacher
could possibly say to you.

14 | DOES GOD NEED YOUR HELP?

A s I have explained, there are two main groups of fallen beings, the violent ones and the deceptive ones. The violent ones are what most people see as evil, and they truly are hell-bent on destroying human beings and everything positive built on earth. They are absolutely determined to destroy, and they have no reverence for life. You cannot reason with them, you cannot talk them out of destroying because they have crossed a line where no reasoning is possible. Why do they do this? Partly because they enjoy the act itself and partly because they enjoy the sense of power that it gives them. They enjoy having the power to destroy the ideal growth scenario defined by God and the ascended masters.

Even though the presence of the violent fallen beings on earth is clearly something we would like to see come to an end, these beings are not our primary concern. Our main concern is to help you see through the deceptive fallen beings because they are the ones who are preventing the removal of the violent beings from earth. How do they do this? The equation is simple. As long as human beings are willing to fight the violent fallen beings – as long as people resist evil – these beings cannot be removed from the earth. What makes people willing to resist evil? The epic dramas defined by the deceptive fallen beings. It really is that simple.

Is God evil?

The function of the violent fallen beings is to provide such a presence of evil that human beings cannot ignore it and are manipulated into looking for a way out. People get the sense that there is an urgency, meaning they *must* do something. This makes them susceptible to the idea that they must fight evil and the people whom they see as representing evil.

The underlying illusion that is being projected by the deceptive fallen beings is that the presence of evil on this planet proves that something has gone wrong with God's plan. This has been used to argue that God is either incompetent or that God must be evil.

The deceptive fallen beings have projected the image that God is almighty and that God is wholly good. The presence of evil seems to contradict both of these claims. If God is almighty, then God must be able to remove evil from earth. The fact that he has not done so leaves only two options. Either God is not almighty, meaning evil has such power that even God can't remove it. Or God is not willing to remove evil from this planet. If God is not willing to remove evil, how could he be wholly good? How could a good God allow evil to continue and refuse to use his power to remove it?

In order to see through this deception, you need to recognize that the image of God projected by the fallen beings is out of touch with reality. God is neither all-powerful nor good—when good is defined as the opposite of evil. As I have explained several times, God has given self-aware beings free will because that is the only way they can grow in self-aware-ness. God has then set up a universe in which you have max-imum opportunities for exercising your free will without destroying yourself.

The Creator does indeed have the power to eradicate evil on a planet like earth. Or rather, God's representatives have that power, as the Creator itself does not even see the evil on earth. The seven Elohim created this planet and they can at any time wipe the slate clean and remove evil. Doing so would, however, be contrary to the purpose for which the earth was created, namely as a laboratory for self-aware beings to exer-cise their free will and see the results outpictured in the mate-rial realm.

We might say that while the Elohim have the power to remove evil, they have suspended that power, allowing it to be dependent upon the choices of human beings in embodiment. As I have explained, only when a critical mass of human beings had gone into duality were the fallen beings allowed to embody here. They will be removed only when a critical mass choose to rise above duality by refusing to resist evil and turning the other cheek.

The reality that the fallen beings do not want you to know is that it is not God who can remove evil from earth but *you*. The Elohim have the power but not the authority. Human beings have the authority but not the power. What is missing is that a critical mass of human beings give the authority to the ascended masters so that we can remove evil. How can you give us this authority? You cannot give it to us as long as you remain in the dualistic mindset, for this is precisely what allows the continued presence of evil. You can give us the authority only by rising above this mindset, and this means you must rise above the epic dramas and stop resisting evil. Just to be clear, God did not sit up in heaven and make the decision to allow evil to appear on earth. God is not evil but God has allowed everything in the material world to depend upon the choices of beings embodying here. This really cannot be put on a scale with evil at one end and human good at the other. It simply is the way it is. You either accept this with the Christ mind or you reject it with the mind of anti-christ.

Does God need your help

How can you begin to free yourself from the subtleties of the epic dramas? By seeing through the deceptions that underpin them. One of these deceptions is the idea that the presence of evil proves that something has gone wrong with God's plan and this needs to be corrected. However, by the very fact that God has not used his power to remove evil, this proves that God is not capable of removing evil and that means God needs the help of human beings. You therefore need to accept the view of life presented by the fallen beings, including their definition of which beliefs systems and people represent evil. You then need to dedicate your life to either killing the people or proving wrong the belief systems that represent evil.

As you begin to see the fallacy of this idea, you can realize that in a sense God does need your help. You will not give this help by struggling in the epic mindset. You will give it only by completely transcending the epic mindset so that you can do the works that I did of exposing evil without resisting it. There are many people in embodiment on earth today who have reached the level of self-awareness where they are ready to consciously abandon the epic mindset and instead step into the Christ consciousness, demonstrating it openly by challenging evil without fighting it. I hope this book can help some of these people awaken to their highest calling.

15 | THE WORLD MIGHT END

If you have ever been exposed to what is called "high-pressure" sales methods, you will know the psychological mechanism. The goal is to create a sense of urgency, meaning that you have to buy now or lose a unique opportunity that will never come back. As mentioned before, the goal is to get you to make rash decisions that you would never make if you took time to step back and look at the situation from a larger perspective. The sense of urgency narrows your perspective, gives you tunnel vision and forces you to focus on the need to make a decision right now, meaning you must make it with the information you have available now, the information presented to you by the sales person.

The fallen beings invented this tactic and they use it effectively through the epic dramas. One of the subtle ideas projected into the collective consciousness is that the earth might be destroyed or that it could be taken over by the devil. What worse threat is imaginable for human beings? What could create a greater sense of urgency? What better way to force people to make rash decisions based on incomplete knowledge, the knowledge presented by the fallen beings with no external frame of reference?

Could the earth be destroyed?

There is some reality to the claim that a planet could be destroyed. This has happened to a number of planets and some of the fallen beings who have embodied on earth have experienced it first-hand. From that perspective, one could say they are right in warning human beings that this is a possibility. The problem is that it is only a possibility because of the presence of the fallen beings. It only becomes a realistic possibility when a critical number of human beings blindly follow the fallen beings and engage in the epic struggle against other human beings.

It now becomes obvious that the fallen beings are using the threat of the destruction of the earth in order to create urgency and get people to fight each other. They are not seeking to warn people out of the goodness of their hearts. They are seeking to manipulate people through fear, and some of them believe they can avoid having the earth be destroyed. Some of them feel no reverence for the earth as a planet and don't care if it is destroyed. Some would even gain a sense of power from destroying (another) planet.

Let me now give you a realistic assessment from the ascended perspective. Planet earth has recently crossed an important dividing line and it is no longer a possibility that this planet could be destroyed or could self-destruct. This is caused by the fact that a critical number of people in embodiment have risen above the epic mindset to such a degree that certain fallen beings have been taken from the planet. There is no longer any fallen being in embodiment with the momentum of evil that could bring the earth to the point of destruction.

You may have read prophecies of a "third anti-christ" that should supposedly rise in the near future and bring the earth into an all-out war. This potential was there until recently, but it is no longer a possibility. Due to certain people rising to the necessary level of Christhood, the fallen being who could have filled this role has been taken from the earth and will never again be allowed to embody here.

There is no longer a realistic risk that the earth could be destroyed or could be taken over by evil. I am telling you this because I know very well that when people begin to awaken to the spiritual path, they will of necessity expand their awareness of many topics that most people ignore. This will cause spiritual seekers to take prophecy seriously, and many have been sucked into a fear-based spiral, making a variety of unbalanced decisions. The net effect being that many of the people who were on the brink of awakening have actually been pulled even deeper into the epic mindset. Even many ascended master students have been pulled into thinking that they are locked in a to-the-death fight against the dark forces on this planet.

The need for balance

I am telling you this because it is absolutely necessary that the 10,000 people who can manifest full Christhood, and the millions more who can manifest a high degree of it, become consciously aware of the epic dramas and begin to rise above them. It is this awakening process that has brought us to the point where the earth cannot be destroyed. It is only the continuation of this process that will bring the earth to the point were all fallen beings have been removed and The Golden Age of Saint Germain will be manifest.

I need people to take a balanced approach. I need you to let go of the fear that the earth could be destroyed so you rise above the epic dramas and the sense of urgency that you must destroy some form of evil in order to prevent a calamity. I also need you to not swing to the other extreme and stop your efforts to raise your consciousness. The fact that certain fallen beings have been removed from the earth does not mean that all fallen beings have been removed. The fact that the entire planet cannot be destroyed does not mean that the remaining fallen beings could not still wreak quite a bit of havoc. Some of them know their time is short and they are determined to do as much damage as they can as their final hurrah on this planet. Again, you do not counter-act this by fighting these fallen beings but by continuing to raise your consciousness above the epic mindset.

As I have said, there comes a point on the path of Christhood where you cannot go higher unless you recognize the existence of the fallen beings and begin to consciously see through their deception. There also comes a point where you cannot go higher until you consciously acknowledge the need to rise above all desire to fight or oppose the fallen beings. You literally must stop resisting evil, and you must do so out of a conscious, inner recognition of why it is essential to stop resisting evil. I have given you the knowledge you need in order to have this inner realization, and I hope it will one day "click" so that you truly see what I am saying.

I hope you will one day awaken and know that the fallen beings can no longer deceive you because you are wise as a serpent. They can no longer get you to fight them because you have become harmless as a dove. This balance is indeed the higher levels of Christhood.

Could your soul be lost?

Another aspect of the epic mindset is the claim that souls could be lost, including yourself. The lie that has been projected by the fallen beings for a very long time is that souls were created in a state of imperfection and thus they need to be saved.

Again, there is some truth to this but the fallen beings have perverted it as they do with everything.

I have told you that your lifestream originated with your I AM Presence. The Presence formed an extension of itself and sent it into this world. This extension is the Conscious You, which I have said is pure awareness. What I mean with this is that the Conscious You has no inherent characteristics. Your divine individuality is anchored in your I AM Presence and can be expressed through the Conscious You. The wisdom of this is that neither the Conscious You nor your true individuality can be destroyed by anything that happens to you in the material world. The fallen beings literally can never attain power over your I AM Presence, and they only have power over the Conscious You as long as you identify with the outer self—what most people call the soul.

As we have explained, the soul was created by you in response to the conditions you encountered in the material world. The soul is made from the energies in the four levels of the material world so it can be damaged or destroyed by these energies. The soul is designed to respond to the material world, meaning it has – over many lifetimes – acquired a certain individuality and personality. This is not your divine individuality but an individuality created as a reaction to the material world. If this individuality was lost, you would lose nothing and would even gain the awareness of your divine individuality that is right now obscured by the human self.

Take note of an essential fact. Even though your soul is made from the energies in this world, your soul truly is not only energy. In order to grasp this, consider an image projected onto a wall by a slide projector. Your soul is a set of images held in the four levels of your lower mind, and these images cause energy to take on a certain form. The images are not permanent but are constantly being projected onto the basic energy, the Ma-ter light. If an image in the mind was changed, one or all of your four lower bodies would change instantly. That is why it was possible for me to generate an instant healing of people's physical bodies, and such healing is possible for you as well.

Most people have allowed their egos and a variety of spirits to form and project the images that define their souls. It is possible for the Conscious You to take back its responsibility for defining the images of your soul. Doing this consciously is what the path to Christhood is all about. Right now, your ego and a group of spirits are to some degree defining your soul images. They can only see the conditions in the material universe so they have no way to defend themselves against the lies of the fallen beings. Each spirit in your being is defined based on a specific lie; it is defined in response to this lie. The spirits are therefore open doors whereby the prince of this world has something in you whereby he can control you.

Your soul is made from the energies and the images of this world, meaning it is a tool that the fallen beings can use to control the Conscious You. They can do so as long as the Conscious You refuses to be conscious. You can – at any time – take back your responsibility to be conscious and thereby take command over your life. You might remember that in an earlier discourse [In the book *Freedom From Ego Games*] I said that there are certain decisions that can be made only by the Conscious You. The devil does not have the power to destroy your soul—only the Conscious You has the power to do this. That is why the fallen beings must deceive you.

Why fallen beings use deception

Ask yourself why the serpent in the Garden of Eden had to deceive Eve instead of simply overpowering her? It is because the violent fallen beings do not have the power to destroy your soul. They can indeed attack and kill your physical body, but this does not destroy your soul. It does, however, force you to react to their attacks, and this is where the deceptive fallen beings come in. They seek to deceive you into reacting to the violent fallen beings through the consciousness of duality, instead of reconnecting to your I AM Presence and letting the reaction come from there. The overall lie of the fallen beings is that when you are in physical embodiment, you *must* react to them and you must do so through the outer self, the soul.

The path to Christhood is not – as even many ascended master students have come to believe – a process of perfecting your soul so it can gain entry into heaven. I told Nicodemus that only the "man" who descended from heaven can ascend back to heaven. That "man" is the Conscious You and the soul must simply be allowed to die in order for you to follow me into the ascended state. I realize this can be confusing at first because so many spiritual teachings, even some previous ascended master teachings, talk about souls being saved or ascending. That is why we decided, as a link in the chain of our ongoing, progressive revelation, to give the teachings about the Conscious You as a part of your being that cannot be destroyed and thus can escape any and all schemes thought up by the fallen beings. The Conscious You becomes free from these schemes by dismissing each of the spirits in your soul vehicle, eventually giving up the last ghost of the ego itself.

Let us return to the original premise that the soul can be lost. We now see that the soul can be lost in the sense that it can gradually come to be made up of so many lower energies and spirits that it can no longer embody in a physical body on earth but gravitates to a lower realm, even a realm similar to the fiery hell seen by various people through the ages. Contrary to what the fallen beings project, this does not happen by the devil forcefully taking over your soul. It happens only because the Conscious You refuses to be conscious and thus allows the ego and a set of spirits to control your life.

The devil can indeed force the ego and the spirits into a progressively lower state of consciousness. This process is never irreversible and the Conscious You can at any time awaken and take back control.

True salvation

The claim that the soul can be lost is used primarily as another scare tactic. The claim is that there is a real threat that the devil could take over your soul, but there is a defense against this threat. That defense is to follow the path to salvation defined by the fallen beings. How could your soul be lost? Only if you blindly followed the fallen beings. Their overall goal is to get you to follow them blindly. They use the scare tactic as a way to get you to follow them blindly while thinking this will guarantee your salvation. Do I need to say it can never work?

What is the true path to salvation or rather the ascension? It is to realize that the Conscious You descended as pure awareness. In order to interact with the physical body and the material world, the Conscious You gradually built a very complex soul vehicle. This vehicle was first based on a limited self-awareness and a limited awareness of the material world. It gradually became expanded but at some point a shift occurred when you decided to experiment with the consciousness of separation. This caused the soul vehicle to become very complex with a multitude of spirits designed to deal with a variety of situations, especially the challenges presented by the fallen beings. This soul vehicle is now so complex and "sophisticated" that it literally believes it has a life of its own. The ego is convinced that it is a real being and that it can one day make the soul so "spiritual" that it will be accepted into heaven. This is a complete illusion. Only the Conscious You can ascend, and it can do so only when it again becomes pure awareness. How can this happen? Only by the Conscious You becoming conscious, seeing why it created a certain spirit and then consciously letting it go.

The process of the ascension is not a process of perfecting the soul. It is a process of systematically dismantling the soul until the Conscious You again sees itself as pure awareness. The Conscious You now becomes an open door for the I AM Presence because it has realized that: "I can of mine own self do nothing. It is the father within me who doeth the work." The soul cannot be perfected, it must be allowed to die so that the Conscious You can be reborn into accepting its immortal nature. This happens when the Conscious You accepts that nothing in this world has changed or corrupted the Conscious You.

The lie of irreparable damage

Another subtle idea projected through the epic dramas is that you could do or experience something in this world so terrible that it would damage you so severely that the damage could never be undone. This is a very deceptive lie that has been projected into the collective consciousness in many subtle ways. One of the more obvious ones is the concept of original sin, which even says that God created you in an imperfect state.

The real effect of this lie is to pacify you because it seems as if you do not have the power to free yourself from what has happened in the past. You could choose to go into a situation but you cannot choose to get out of it. You can now see why this is a lie. In a sense we can say that the soul vehicle can be damaged beyond repair. It is possible to create so many spirits that are warring each other, each one being so wounded by the warring, that it is virtually impossible to heal it again. To help you understand this, consider the physical body. It can be wounded but many wounds can be healed by the body itself. The soul vehicle also has a certain ability to heal itself, which is why most people have experienced that time will heal the effects of a traumatic experience. It can be viable to pursue soul healing, or soul retrieval, as a way to get back some sense of wholeness.

In the long run, no amount of soul healing will secure your ascension. Soul healing can pave the way for the Conscious You awakening to the fact that it has the ability to overcome a past trauma not simply by healing the soul but by giving up the wounded aspect of the soul. As I said, the soul can be so severely wounded that it cannot repair itself. The only way out of this kind of trauma is for the Conscious You to look at the situation and begin to dismiss the spirits that cause the wound in the soul. The wounded soul cannot be healed, but it can be allowed to die and then the Conscious You will be free of the effects of the wound.

You now see that there is always a way out of any situation you have experienced. You can always rise above your past, as long as you are willing to let go of the soul parts that were damaged in the past. You do this partly by coming to see the illusion that created specific spirits and then dismissing the illusion through the Christ mind. You also do it by invoking spiritual light to transmute the energies that formed the soul. Once you have rebalanced the energies and dismissed the illusions, that part of the soul will have died and the damage has been erased as if it never existed. Truly, it never did exist anywhere but in your own soul vehicle. It had no objective existence in God, which is why God has said: "I will remember their sins no more."

16 | DOES THE CHRIST HAVE OPINIONS?

I want you to seriously consider whether a Christed being has human opinions. You have likely been brought up to think you need to have opinions about everything, including political issues, religious issues and how other people live their lives. Many spiritual seekers have experienced that as they discovered the path they became aware of a lot of issues that most "normal" people do not even think about. This has caused many sincere spiritual seekers to formulate a set of opinions beyond what most people have. Many even think that having these opinions and holding on to them is part of their spiritual growth. Why did I tell people not to judge after appearances?

It is indeed a subtle effect of the epic dramas that you need to formulate an opinion about everything you encounter in life. What is an opinion? It is often a black-and-white judgment based on a very one-sided view of the issue or of other people. It causes people to judge an issue based on limited knowledge, and once the judgment is formed, the ego thinks it is a matter of life or death never to change it or have it proven wrong.

What is the effect of this? It causes people to identify themselves with their opinions. In reality, you are the Conscious You and you are pure awareness. Pure awareness is beyond any human opinion or judgment. A human opinion is formed in the outer self, but the Conscious You does not become the outer self and thus it does not become the opinions of the outer self. It is not a matter of life or death for the Conscious You if an opinion is proven wrong. It is only a matter of life and death for the spirit who was formed to defend that opinion. Do you really want to have your conscious attention eaten up by an inconsequential effort to defend the opinions of spirits that have no real life in them?

The quest never to be wrong

Another effect of the epic dramas is that they project that it is epically important for a human being to have the right opinions. Being wrong is disastrous in an epic way so it is essential that you are never proven wrong. What does it mean to never be proven wrong? It means that one of your opinions is never proven wrong.

What have I said is the characteristic of the duality consciousness? It always has two opposing polarities. This means that any opinion which is formulated based on the duality consciousness will have an opposite. As long as an opinion has an opposite, it can always be proven wrong. When you adopt a dualistic opinion, you are actually allowing a spirit to enter your soul vehicle. There will always be another spirit which has the opposite opinion of the one you adopted. You cannot avoid being affected by the conflict between these two spirits.

The fallen beings have managed to trick most people into a never-ending game of seeking to never be proven wrong by defending your opinions. It is inevitable that some other people will have adopted the exact opposite of your opinion so your opinion will always be threatened by its opposite. You now have to prove that the opinions of other people are wrong in order to defend your own opinion. As a quick look at history will prove, there is literally no end to this game. It will consume your attention right up until the Conscious You awakens and becomes wise as a serpent and harmless as a dove. Meaning that you see the fallacy of needing to have opinions and you give up all desire to be proven right among men, seeking instead to be right with God.

The fallen beings have created a very aggressive force that does attack anyone who dares to express Christhood in this world. Most of the lifestreams who have the potential to manifest Christhood at this time came to earth in order to help raise this planet beyond the fallen consciousness. When you first came here, the fallen beings knew you were a threat to their control so they attacked you viciously. Their aim was to in any way possible prove you wrong by criticizing you, ridiculing you and putting you down. They would literally do anything – including lying in all kinds of ways – in order to prove you wrong.

What was their purpose? It was to get you to feel that in order to prove that they were wrong for making you look wrong, you had to engage in an effort to prove them wrong. The violent fallen beings pull you into a dualistic game by presenting you with a situation where it seems like you have to kill them in order to prevent them from killing you. The deceptive fallen beings seek to pull you into the game of proving them wrong in order to avoid having them prove you wrong. If you fall for this deception, you are now caught in a drama to prove others wrong rather than being an open door for the light from your I AM Presence. The light can indeed raise the world whereas proving others wrong will never raise the world.

Take note of what I have said about duality. Every opinion has an opposite, meaning there is no final argument, there is no absolute truth. You will not promote the growth of the earth by proving the devil wrong. You will promote the growth of this planet only by raising yourself above the entire dualistic game of proving one dualistic illusion right by proving another dualistic illusion wrong. When you have pulled that beam from your own eye, you will then see clearly and can now seek to help others do the same.

Witnessing versus opinions

Am I thereby saying that the Christ never has opinions? That is exactly what I am saying. The Christ mind is beyond duality and thus holds no dualistic opinions. Does that mean a Christed being should keep his or her mouth shut and never engage in any kind of debate? It does not, as you will see demonstrated by me 2,000 years ago. It does mean that you do not engage in a debate on the terms for the debate defined by the fallen beings. What are those terms? That any statement must be right or wrong according to some standard in this world, a standard defined by the duality consciousness. The effect being that you engage in the debate for the purpose of proving right one idea and proving wrong any opposing idea. You may even take pleasure in raising yourself by proving other people wrong.

It is a sad fact that many people have adopted a very judgmental attitude towards other people based on opinions. They have identified themselves based on their opinions and they identify others based on their opinions. Everything now happens at the level of opinions, which is a very superficial level. You will see that many religious people are extremely judgmental towards the members of other religions. Many political people are judgmental towards members of other political persuasions. Even many atheists are quick to point out the fallacy of religious persecution while being extremely judgmental of religious people.

What is lost in this game of judgment? What is lost is the humanity that can form the basis of mutual respect between people. When you judge someone else, you do not truly see them as other human beings. The Nazis judged the Jews based on an absolutist standard, meaning that in the eyes of believers in Nazi ideology, the Jews had lost their humanity. That is why some Germans could do to the Jews what they could never have done to members of their own group.

Judgment makes you believe that some people are fundamentally different from you. Perhaps God created them different or nature made them different, but they are so different that normal humanitarian concerns do not apply to them. You feel no kinship with the people you judge, and thus you can do to them what you could never do to those of your own kin.

Beyond this, the judgment games obscure the basic reality of life, namely that all life is one. This is a reality that can be seen only with the Christ mind, and the judgment games take you completely out of the Christ mind.

If the Christ mind has no opinions, how does it look at life? It simply witnesses what it sees without judging it in any way. The Christ mind is in oneness with God and all life. It can instantly feel whether an idea or action is coming from oneness or from separation. It instantly recognizes what comes from separation but it still does not judge it. It might indeed seek to express a different perspective, perhaps by witnessing to a higher reality or by making people aware that one or both opinions in a debate are out of touch with reality. It may even challenge people's opinions or behavior but it never does so in order to put people down. It does so in order to free them from illusions and help them see the reality that they are all part of the Body of God. The Christ mind may seek to help you see that your opinion is not the highest possible, but it never seeks to prove *you* wrong. It knows you are more than your opinions and it seeks to help you reconnect to that fact.

Opinions versus reality

Take note of the fundamental difference between opinions and the witnessing of the Christ mind. Opinions exist in the human self, which is by nature separated from oneness. When you look at life through the filter of the human self, there is a gap, a separation between you, the subject, and the object you are observing. You can never overcome that gap except when the Conscious You steps outside the human self and reconnects to pure awareness. Once you are reconnected to your I AM Presence, you can look at life on earth as your Presence looks at it, meaning you can see the underlying oneness between all appearances on earth.

When you judge after appearances, you judge based on the illusion that different forms are separate. When you see with the clarity of the Christ mind, you see the underlying oneness behind all appearances. That is why I told people not to judge after appearances.

The Christ mind is what the ancients called "gnosis," and, as mentioned, it means oneness between the knower and the known. It happens when the Conscious You returns to pure awareness whereby the separation between subject and object is dissolved.

Imagine that you are watching the performance of a puppet theater. The human self is like watching the performance without any awareness that there is anything behind the screen. You think the puppets are real and you might become very judgmental towards the villain. The Christ mind sees behind the screen and sees that the puppets are controlled by people and that what the puppets do on the stage has no ultimate reality or consequence. The person controlling the villain is not a bad person but is simply playing a role, a role that he can step out of at any time.

When you look at life on earth through the filter of the human mind, you think people are separated and that some people really are bad, judged by their actions or opinions. The Christ mind sees that every human being has a Conscious You that is still pure awareness and is part of the Body of God. It also sees that a person's opinions and actions are controlled by spirits that have no ultimate reality and thus have no ultimate consequence for the fate of the world. The Christ also sees that even if a person is now fully identified with the human self, the Conscious You can at any time step out of that and reconnect to who it really is.

Proving others wrong

This leads to a fundamental difference in approach. Most human beings have bought into another illusion created by the fallen beings. This illusion says that you have to free people from their erroneous ways. The way to do this is to prove their opinions and beliefs to be wrong in an absolute way. The underlying assumption is that if you prove an opinion wrong, the person will see how right you are and will then snap out of his or her identification with the opinion.

Based on what I have told you about spirits, you can now begin to see the fallacy of this approach. Why is the other person holding a given opinion? Because he has accepted into his soul vehicle the spirit that is programmed to promote and defend that opinion. The person is now looking at life through that spirit and literally cannot see anything beyond what the spirit is letting through.

Why do you hold a certain opinion and why do other people hold opposite opinions? Most people have fallen for the fallen illusion that you are not holding an opinion but have the absolute truth. The deeper reality is that you are holding your opinion because you have accepted the spirit that is the polar opposite of the other person's spirit.

When you argue with the other person, you are presenting a view of the issue that is colored by your spirits, meaning it has filtered out any contrary evidence. You are completely convinced that what you are saying is a higher truth. When the other person hears what you are saying, it will be filtered through *his* spirit, and it will filter out or invalidate all contrary evidence. What you say seems completely valid to you because it is filtered by *your* spirit. The same words seem completely invalid to the other person because it is filtered by *his* spirit.

There literally will never be a meeting of the minds because the two spirits are programmed to prevent this. The arguments you come up with based on your spirit will never convince the other spirit. Neither spirit is self-conscious so they cannot step back and change their opinion.

The net result is that you feel the other person is rejecting your arguments and even rejecting you. This leads you to respond with negative feelings that you might even direct at the other person in order to make him feel bad so he will accept what you are saying. The other person might respond by directing negative feelings at you, and the two of you now form the beginning of a negative spiral that can become increasingly intense over time. You can see such negative spirals block the communication between people, from married couples to business associates, political figures and even nations and civilizations.

A loving approach

What confuses the issue is that it is sometimes possible to convince another person that you are right and that he needs to change his opinion. This does not happen through spirits. If another person changes his opinion, it is because his Conscious You has managed to step outside of the spirit and get in touch with his basic humanity. From this inner connection – however it is perceived by the person – it is indeed possible to change your opinion. It is never possible as long as you are fully identified with a spirit.

This gives you a new perspective. Many people, even many spiritual people, take a sense of pride in being good at convincing other people. In many cases, this is not because they are superior but because the people they convince are superior—from a spiritual viewpoint. The people who take pride in convincing others are often fully identified with a certain spirit and they are interacting with other people through that spirit. The people who are convinced are more in touch with their own humanity, and that is why they are willing to change their opinions. This is not true for all cases, but it is true for some and it should give you pause if you take pride in convincing others.

Here is another perspective. What is the real way to get another person to let go of a limiting opinion? It is to seek to help the other person reconnect to his or her basic humanity, the sense of pure awareness. This is not achieved by proving wrong the other person's opinion but by making him or her realize that you love and respect them regardless of their opinions.

What will it take for you to perform this service to life? It will take that you have first reconnected to your own basic humanity by overcoming your identification with your opinions. You must first pull the spirit from your own eye before you can help another person do the same. My hope is that these teachings can awaken spiritual people to their highest potential on earth, namely to be an open door for the I AM Presence. By engaging in personal and public debates from the oneness of the Christ mind, even a relatively small number of people can be successful in changing the tone and focus of public debate. Truly, anyone who will make an effort to go through this shift will feel that his or her efforts will be greatly multiplied by my momentum and that of other ascended masters. Prove me herewith, sayeth the Lord, and I shall pour you out a blessing so that there shall not be room enough to receive it.

The epic dramas make you think you are or have to be God, meaning you have to know everything and provide everything yourself. They even make you think that you have to be the Christ, and for most people this seems very difficult. They see a gap between themselves and Christhood and the gap remains no matter what they do. The trick is to realize that the Conscious You can of its own self do nothing. It is pure awareness and cannot act in this world. It can act either through an outer self that it has created or it can act by letting the I AM Presence be the doer through its open door.

The key to fulfilling your mission is to realize that you can never do so as a separate self. You can do so only when you realize that you are a co-creator and that the I AM Presence is the true doer. Your role is to be the open door, and in order to be open, you need to dismantle the outer self that stands in the way of the spirit expressing itself freely through you. Only in oneness with your Presence will you feel fullness and completeness. The separate self will forever give you emptiness, no matter how much power it attains in this world.

Free will once again

Go back to my description of how people argue with each other through opposing spirits and build a negative spiral that takes over their relationship. The epic mindset makes use of the frustration many people feel by arguing that this proves that free will was a mistake. After all, since you have the absolute truth, it is only in the other person's best interest that he comes to accept your truth. It would obviously be best if you had the power to force his will into accepting what is best for him. It is necessary or better to take away or restrict free will so that the epic goal of saving people and the world can be fulfilled. This would also prevent people from making the kind of choices from which there is – claims the fallen beings – no way back. Is it not better to take away people's free will before they make choices that lead to the destruction of the entire planet?

Why take away free will when free will allows you to make a choice that takes you completely beyond any choice made in the past? The magic of free will is that there is no choice you could possibly make that cannot be erased by another choice. As long as you know your will is free, you can undo any past choice. Nothing is permanent and nothing can hold you back.

The only problem with free will is that the fallen beings have managed to make people believe it is not truly free. You think you are limited by your own past choices, that you could have done something so bad that you can never rise above it. You cannot simply make a new choice that erases past choices.

The magic of the Christ consciousness is that when you do make a choice from the Christ mind, it will indeed completely erase a choice made from the mind of anti-christ. This is the true meaning of Christ as the redeemer who removes the sins of the world. What removes your sins is not me as an external savior. It is when the Christ becomes internal and you make the choice to rise above the consciousness in which you chose to sin. It is when you make a Christic choice that your sins will be white as wool instead of red as scarlet.

Again, the fallen beings only want you to restrict your free will because that is the only way they can control you. The Christ knows that regardless of the choices you have made in the past, regardless of how terrible the consequences have been here on earth, you can at any time make a choice to raise yourself above your past choices. The Christ is in complete acceptance of free will as the only way for self-aware beings to raise their self-awareness.

You may in the past have chosen to accept the illusions of the fallen beings. Nothing in the present prevents you from awakening to the reality of what you have done and then changing it with a choice based on the Christ mind.

The fallen beings and your own ego will try to make you believe that admitting you have made dualistic choices in the past will cause you unbearable pain. Only the spirits and your ego can feel this pain. The Conscious You feels no pain when it reconnects to pure awareness. The reality is that seeing the limitations of a past choice will instantly set you free from that choice. Why is this so? How can you come to see the limitations of a choice based on duality? Surely, the mind of anti-christ cannot show you those limitations. Only the mind of Christ can show you the limitations, and once you connect to the mind of Christ, you will be free from your past choices.

Wont you invite the Christ mind into your being and allow it to wash white all of your past choices? This is the ultimate use of free will for a human being. Only when you become the bride of Christ will you reclaim your freedom of will.

17 | CLAIMING YOUR INNOCENCE

The most subtle and thus potentially most devastating effect of the epic dramas is that they rob you of your innocence. If you try to center your attention in your heart, you will notice that deep within your being is the sense that you have lost something, perhaps even a sense of irretrievable loss.

That sense of loss comes from the fact that the Conscious You can never quite forget that it has lost the most precious gift with which it came into this world. We might call it innocence, but I have also called it pure awareness, an awareness that is not colored by the value-laden polarities of the mind of anti-christ.

Most of the people who will be open to this book are those who did not come into being as new co-creators on planet earth. You have come from other planets or from other realms and you have descended to earth on what we might call a rescue mission. Even using the word "rescue mission" is dangerous because it so easily ties in to the epic mindset.

Christ and judgment

Consider how my coming to this earth has been presented as the most epic act ever, namely the descent of the *only* son of God on the ultimate rescue mission to wrestle the world from the hands of the devil and prevent all people from being condemned to an eternity in hell. In reality, this was not at all the purpose for my coming, and if you have read the first books in this series, you will already know why: Free will is the ultimate law.

The fallen beings are the ones who want to force the free will of human beings. Those who represent Christ will never seek to force people's free will, for we know it is only through making choices that people grow, and growth in self-awareness is the purpose of the universe. We might challenge people to let go of beliefs and attitudes that restrict their free will, making it less than free, but even this is not done through force.

All that a Christed beings ever does or will do is to be who it is. As a Christed being, you are the open door for your I AM Presence. You no longer have an outer self which evaluates what should or should not be done based on some standard or the conditions found on earth. You are letting your I AM Presence shine its light wherever it listeth and you have no opinion or judgment about what should come from the Presence. Neither do you have any opinion or judgment about how other people should react or how they do react. You are not adapting the light to them deliberately based on a mental image, although the expression of light will be somewhat influenced by the fact that you have grown up in a certain culture and you express yourself in the conceptual language of that culture.

This is innocence. You do not judge what comes from the I AM Presence. You do not judge what other people should do with it. You do not judge what they actually do and then let your outer mind set up restrictions for how the light should be expressed in the future. You are allowing the I AM Presence – who has the infinitely broader perspective from the spiritual realm – to judge what it sends forth. You allow the Presence to judge what happens here on earth.

I know I said that the father judges no man but has committed all judgment to the son. I know that I also called the I AM Presence "father." However, I used the word "father" to refer to both the Creator and your Presence. The son is the Christ mind, and the Creator has given it to that mind to judge. The I AM Presence uses the Christ mind in order to "judge" what you encounter on earth. When the Conscious You fulfills its role of being the open door (and nothing more), you no longer have an outer self that judges what you encounter on earth. You remain centered in pure awareness and you simply observe, you witness what is happening without judging. You have no human opinions or expectations—and thus no pain or suffering. Every situation is new and you meet it with a clean state of mind. You have become as a little child.

The I AM Presence does "judge" but it does not do so based on the dualistic standard of the fallen beings. You can experience the evaluation of your I AM Presence, but you can do so only when you have systematically let the human self die. If you have not done so, you will – often without being aware of what you are doing – impose subtle judgments from the human mind upon the Presence. You will have a subtle desire for what the Presence should or should not express through you. You will also want the Presence (or the ascended masters or God) to validate and confirm the judgments of your ego. The ascended masters will never do this, but there are plenty of false hierarchy impostors who will validate any judgment of your ego. I have said that those who attain Christhood may indeed serve to bring forth a judgment of the fallen beings so that these beings can no longer embody on earth. This judgment is not brought about by you forming an evaluation with the human mind and then thinking God will validate your view of another person. The judgment of Christ is brought about when you attain innocence and allow your Presence to express light that the fallen beings then reject or put down. It is in this act of rejecting the light of Christ that the fallen beings are judged.

I trust you see the vital difference. The fallen beings are not judged based on choices *you* make. They are judged based on choices *they* make. You are simply being the open door for the light that "forces" them to choose this day whom they will serve.

As a Christed being you never force the will of other people, you never force them to make a specific choice. You are simply an open door for the light of the Presence, and when this light is expressed on earth, no one (especially not the fallen beings) can ignore it. They must either accept or reject the light, and their choice is their judgment. According to the Law of Free Will, you do not have the right to force anyone from the mind of anti-christ. You do have the right to force someone to react to the light of Christ being expressed through you. The reason being that the choices of other people to go into the mind of anti-christ can never override or set aside your right to go into the mind of Christ and becoming an open door for that mind to shine its light into the dark dungeons of earth.

The importance of innocence

You now see that everything I have said about the ego and everything I have said about epic dramas have led up to this point. I hope I can help you see the need to claim your ability to be in embodiment on earth while being in complete innocence.

I know well that many spiritual people are motivated by dreams of acquiring special powers that will enable them to win a victory for the light and perhaps even destroy the forces of darkness. I hope you can now see that the ultimate power is the light of the Christ mind. This light can stream through you only when you become a completely open door. When you rise to the higher levels of the spiritual path, you need to make this your conscious goal and put away childish things.

You become an open door only by claiming your innocence, namely the ability to be confronted with all that the forces of anti-christ, the fallen beings and human beings can throw at you and yet remaining in pure awareness. You are not disturbed by anything and you do not react to anything from the human mind. You remain centered in simply witnessing and then allowing your I AM Presence to decide how to respond.

You now see that there are two levels of innocence. When a new co-creator first descends into embodiment, it has innocence but it also has a point-like self-awareness. Your task is to expand the sphere of your self-awareness by becoming aware of more and more of what is manifest in the unascended sphere where you embody. In the ideal scenario, you will do this while retaining and even expanding your connection to your I AM Presence. You will become more aware while actually becoming more innocent.

It is possible to go through the process of growth without ever encountering fallen beings. You will be confronted with the initiations of the separate consciousness, but if you do not become lost in it, you will never have to embody on a planet where fallen beings embody. Obviously, you do find yourself in embodiment on a planet where there are fallen beings. You may have come here because you were deceived by the fallen beings to go into duality. You may have volunteered to embody here in order to provide a counter-balance to the fallen beings. Either way, the result is the same. In past lifetimes, you did become blinded by the fallen consciousness, as has happened to all of us who have ever embodied on this planet.

Regardless of how it happened, the reality is that you have been deeply affected by the fallen consciousness. Your task as a spiritual student and as a Christed being in the making is to claim a new form of innocence. I said that in the original innocence you do not have an awareness of fallen beings and their mindset. On earth your challenge is to claim a state of innocence that does include the awareness of the fallen beings and all that has been manifested out of the consciousness of anti-christ. Your challenge is to become wise as a serpent and harmless as a dove. Your challenge is to be aware of the fallen beings and what they have done on this planet so you can serve as an instrument for exposing it. At the same time you must attain a state of innocence in which you do not react to the fallen beings by becoming pulled into the epic mindset and the epic battle.

Christhood requires awareness and innocence

There are many people on earth today who have increased their awareness of what is happening behind the facade. Some have studied so-called conspiracy theories and some have studied spiritual teachings, including the teachings of the ascended masters. Many people have expanded their awareness, either of the existence of fallen beings or at least of what has been done to manipulate humankind. In itself, this is not Christhood.

It has the potential to become Christhood, but it can do so only when these people claim the new form of innocence while retaining their awareness. Becoming aware of the fallen beings and what they have done is a necessary first step.

I completely understand that as you begin to expand your awareness and come to know what most "normal" people do not or will not know, you will go through a period where you become disturbed, even frightened. The purpose of our teachings on non-duality is to help you move through that phase as quickly as possible.

When you continue to expand your awareness, including your self-awareness, you see that the fallen beings might seem powerful on earth, but their power is a house built on sand. They have power only through the mind of anti-christ, meaning their power is based on an illusion. Their power is not real and its appearance has no more power than what human beings give to it, either through physical submission or by submitting to the illusions. When you see this, you see that nothing on earth is ultimately real and nothing has power over the Conscious You. Then why be afraid of the fallen beings, who truly have no more power over you than what you give them?

How do you give them power? Partly by being unaware of their actions or by being deceived. Have you not now expanded your awareness so you are aware of many of their lies? What is missing is that you expand your awareness so you become aware of their unreality whereby you can finally pull yourself out of the epic mindset and the belief that you have to adapt to them, even that you have to adapt the expression of your light to them. When you become both wise as a serpent and harmless as a dove, *that* is when the fallen beings will truly have no power over you.

Knowing everything that is wrong on earth while remaining blinded by the epic mindset is not Christhood. Christhood is when you can stand trial before the fallen beings in their self-defined courts and not defend yourself but allow them to bring about their own judgment.

Expressing your light

If you have a dark room, how do you get rid of the darkness? No matter how much you know about the darkness, you still cannot remove it. There is a subtle belief that if you give people the full knowledge of how they are being manipulated by the fallen beings, then they will automatically wake up and throw off the yoke. This is not so.

Imagine people who have grown up in a dark cave and have never seen the light. You can tell them everything that is wrong with the darkness and you can tell them about the light, but none of this will have an ultimate effect. How does knowing about the darkness help you remove the darkness?

What must you do to remove the darkness from the cave? You must open up a doorway so that light from outside the cave can shine into it. When people have lived their whole lives, even many lifetimes, in the darkness of the mind of anti-christ, they simply don't have a frame of reference for seeing what it really is. The moment a dark light shines into their cave, they no longer intellectually understand the darkness, they actually *see* the darkness for the first time.

The condition on earth today is that the vast majority of human beings have never seen anything outside the mind of anti-christ, which means they simply do not see it. Only when you see a ray of the Christ light, will you be able to see the mind of anti-christ. Only then will you be able to see it as something that is not natural, something that is not real, something that is not necessary.

The real way to be the Christ in action is not to simply expose the problems with the darkness. It is indeed important to expose problems, but it will ultimately come to naught unless there is also an expression of the Christ light. This will increase the level of light in the cave of the collective consciousness. This will enable people to see something they cannot see today.

You can indeed increase your awareness of the darkness, but this is not Christhood. Only when you also become an open door for the light, will you be the Christ in action. How do you become an open door for the light? By claiming the new form of innocence that does not come from ignorance about the fallen beings. It comes from knowing about them and also knowing their unreality.

By knowing their unreality, you can come to see that the expression of your light and creativity should never be adapted to the conditions that the fallen beings have defined here on earth. The light is real but the conditions are unreal. Do not let that which is real adapt to that which is unreal, for it ties you to unreality. The fallen beings have managed to rob most people of their innocence, and they have done this by making them believe that their creative expression should – indeed, must – be adapted to the standard defined by the fallen beings.

Most people have been tricked into letting the fallen beings become their frame of reference. In reality, your only frame of reference should be your I AM Presence. The representatives of Christ have only one aim, namely to help you free yourself from the yoke of the ego and the serpentine illusions so you can reclaim your innocence. As long as your frame of reference is something on earth, your happiness and inner peace will be dependent upon something on earth—where everything is dominated by duality and everything has an opposite. When your frame of reference is beyond earth, your inner state will depend on the unchanging peace and joy of your I AM Presence. That is when you attain conscious innocence. Claim that innocence and then let your light shine upon all.

The basic choice
for any spiritual student is this:
Do you want to project and reject,
or do you want to understand
and expand?

18 | GIVE UP CHANGING THE FALLEN BEINGS

NOTE: This discourse was given as a spoken dictation.

Jesus: I am the ascended master Jesus Christ, and I wish to give you a different perspective on the Easter story. Instead of focusing on the resurrection, I wish to focus on the fact that I was arrested by the powers that be, the power elite, and that I was imprisoned, that I was humiliated in various ways, that I was judged by them, and that I was eventually executed after being tortured.

This is a parallel to what all of you experience when you are in physical embodiment and when you begin to approach your Christhood. It will not, of course, take the same physical form where you will also be nailed to a cross made of wood, but it will take some form or other, perhaps not even physical. Perhaps you will be persecuted and crucified in the emotional realm, the mental realm or the identity realm.

But there will be some persecution even in the physical. It is simply part of the deal, my beloved, when you volunteer to embody on earth. It has always been so since the fall of this planet and the first fallen beings embodied here, for they will attack those who are the Holy Innocents. They will attack those who are the light bringers, those who dare let their light so shine before men, those who will not hide it beneath the conditions defined by the fallen beings.

The awakening is drawing closer

These fallen beings form a force on this earth, and in their blindness – their spiritual blindness – they have such spiritual pride and arrogance that they believe they control life. They believe that they can shut out the Christ and the Christ light from this planet. I came 2,000 years ago to prove them wrong. I did prove them wrong, for there was a group of fallen beings that was taken out of embodiment back then and they will never again embody here.

You may look at Christianity as it has unfolded over the past 2,000 years and you may see that it has not produced millions of people with the same level of Christ consciousness. You may think that even though the fallen beings could not kill me by killing my body, they have still killed my example, they have killed the church, the religion that claims to represent me.

But I tell you, it is not so for there are still the 10,000 and the millions more who are ready to manifest Christhood in this embodiment and they are coming ever closer. Some have found the teachings we have given through this and other messengers. Some have known from within or even through a teaching not given directly by the ascended masters.

People are beginning to awaken and realize that we are standing before a monumental shift in consciousness on this planet and that they have a role in it. In order to fulfill that role they need to transcend that sense of self, they need to transcend themselves, their former limitations and conditions.

Being in a close relationship with fallen beings

I would give you a deeper teaching than I have given before about how you deal with the fallen beings. There are many of those who volunteered to come to earth with Sanat Kumara, or after Sanat Kumara came, who have volunteered, as Venus explained, [See the book *The Song of Life Healing Matrix.*] to give an opportunity to those who are trapped in the fallen consciousness. Many of the spiritual people on earth have embodied in close relationships with those in the fallen consciousness. It may be parents, spouses, children, family members or people that you otherwise associate with. It is often people where you have a very close physical relationship that can even be a physical dependence.

This is a common scenario because when you are in your last embodiment or close to what is your last embodiment, you want to pass the initiations and you want to pass them quickly. There is no better way to pass the last initiations than to be in such close association in your personal relationships with a fallen being. Not all of you are meant to stand up to the fallen ones in a public setting, as I did. Many of you have, at least as an initial step, chosen to embody with fallen beings in these close, personal relationships.

What is the key to passing this initiation? First of all it is that you do not allow the fallen beings to change you to the point where you deny your Christhood. You will often have to hold back your Christhood in order to even associate with the fallen beings, but this does not mean that you have to compromise it to the point where you cannot express it—when you have fulfilled divine cycles and you no longer need to be concerned about adapting and maintaining a relationship. What then is the key to moving to the next level of initiation?

In many cases you have a deep sense that you are meant to help this other person. You may, over time, begin to see certain patterns in that person's psychology, and you may see that the person is not willing to look at this, is not able to look at this, and will not acknowledge that he or she has a problem even though you may have demonstrated how you have transcended yourself many times during the course of the relationship.

This makes it easy for you to come to that point of thinking that you have to change the other person. However, if you allow yourself to believe that you need to change a person who is in the fallen consciousness, you are making your own progress and your ascension dependent on the choices of another self-aware being.

We might say that the person in the fallen consciousness is not truly self-aware at the highest definition of that word. You are making your life dependent on the choices of an unenlightened being who may think that he or she is smart and spiritual, but who is nevertheless trapped in the blindness of the fallen consciousness.

This is something you do not want to do, my beloved. I tell you that many of you who are the spiritual people, many of you who have that Holy Innocence buried somewhere deep within your hearts, you need to consider that perhaps it is time for you to look at the people in your circle of influence, to begin to identify who are the ones in the fallen consciousness and therefore begin to look at how your relationships with these people have affected yourself, your view of yourself, your view of spirituality, your abilities to express your light, your abilities to do things in the physical.

There is no one in the fallen consciousness who is not trapped in the pattern of wanting to control others, wanting you to be in a co-dependent relationship that you cannot move out of because they have managed to put on you the belief that you are somehow limited, that you should somehow hold yourself back in order to maintain that relationship. They want to keep you trapped, they often even believe that they are the ones who have given you a certain position or a certain ability, and therefore they have some sense of ownership over you.

The initiations of Christhood

Lady Venus has already given instructions in her dictation for *The Song of Life Healing Matrix*, but I wish to have my say on this also. It is indeed the initiation that I had to pass during my arrest, my trial, my crucifixion.

I myself had taken on several people in the fallen consciousness as my personal disciples, most notably Peter who was an original fallen angel. He was a typical example of those who are so trapped in the fallen consciousness and he believed he could tell the Christ, the embodied Christ, what should or should not happen to me, how I should and should not teach him as my disciple.

This, my beloved, is an important sign to watch out for. There are people who believe that they are smarter than the ascended masters. They know better than the ascended masters what the masters should say or what they should do, whom they should chose as a messenger, how they should express themselves.

This you will find in many spiritual movements. You will even find it in many religions where of course those who have taken over the Christian religion believe that they have a right to define how the church of Christ should be. They believe that through the fallen consciousness they can determine how they should represent Christ on earth. They do not represent Christ, for I know them not, those who sit in their council meetings, in their elaborate cathedrals and their palaces, and who think they can determine who should represent Christ.

Look at the new pope, my beloved. A good sign is the humility. Then look at the fact that he comes from a tradition that still will not allow women to have any position in the church. Ask yourself if those who believe they have a right to put down women can truly be said to represent Christ? Nay. No one who puts down women represents Christ, for women are the key to the golden age. Not only women, as a physical sex, but as the representatives of the divine feminine have explained, that all of you see yourselves as part of the divine feminine. How can you do this if you put down women in a physical way? How can you put down women unless you put down your own femininity? If you do not have balance between the masculine and the feminine, how can you represent Christ? Christ did not come to elevate men by putting down women. Christ came to raise up all so that all might have life and that more abundantly.

The sense of ownership of other people

Be careful to recognize the signs of those who have a sense of ownership over you where, as long as you conform to their image of how you should be and how the relationship should be, everything is fine. But when you no longer conform, all of a sudden they turn against you from one moment to the next. They become like the angry mob who first welcomed me when I rode into Jerusalem on a donkey, and then at my trial turned against me and cried: "Barabbas, Barabbas," preferring a murderer to the embodied Christ.

This is a sure sign of those who have put down the Christ in themselves to such a degree that they think they have the right to put down the Christ in others. Not only a right, but an obligation. They even think it is doing God's work that they put down the Christ in others, for they think they can own the Christ in this world. Such is their arrogance.

Look at how many examples you will find from world history of how people have suddenly turned. First, they idolize you and turn you into a hero. Then they put you down and demonize you. This flip-flopping from one extreme to the other is a sure sign of the spiritual blindness that can come only from the fallen consciousness. Where else would it come from, my beloved?

When you see people around you who have this tendency, this sense of ownership over you – and when you know that if you do not conform to their standard, then they will attempt to control you and in all ways put pressure upon you in order to come back into the fold, so to speak – when you see this pattern, you know whom you are dealing with. What then is the key to being free of such beings?

In the beginning you must break free of the relationship. Often this will mean a physical break-up, but it can also be done by you breaking free in consciousness. There are, of course, some relationships that you cannot break up easily, such as that with parents and children. But you can break free in consciousness by realizing that you are not here to submit to these beings.

Do not submit or rebel

I admit that when you first realize that you are not here to submit, it is very easy, and it is almost inevitable, that for a time you go into the opposite extreme and realize that you have to rebel, you have to go against them in order to be free. You even saw this in my own embodiment when I many times engaged the scribes and the Pharisees in heavy debates. I had many of these debates, many more than what you see in the Bible. You saw me overturn the tables on the money changers in the temple.

Do you not see that in the end, when I was captured by them, when I was put on trial, I said nothing? By then I had begun to realize that it was not my personal role to fight against or rebel against the fallen beings. You are not here to submit, but neither are you here to rebel because either action ties you to an action-reaction game with the fallen beings. You do not want to be in an action-reaction game with them for there is no end to it. No ultimate outcome is possible.

The ultimate outcome is the judgment of Christ, but that happens only when you can meet the fallen beings and their accusations with complete non-attachment. That non-attachment can come from only one place: unconditional love. As long as you have conditions, you cannot be non-attached to the fallen beings. There will be something in you that the prince of this world will use to reach in and grab a hold of you and force you into an action-reaction pattern.

Only when you have let go of your conditions, can you be the open door for the love of God, which then is the ultimate judgment. There is no greater judgment than those who are receiving unconditional love and yet reject it and reject the one who is the open door for it, persecute him, crucify him, kill him, ridicule him, mock him in various ways. Or her, of course, as many Christed beings are women in this age.

You cannot convince fallen beings

At my trial I had realized it was not my personal task to convert or change or awaken those in the fallen consciousness. I knew because at that time I had realized that there was nothing I could say that would convince the Sanhedrin, or even the

Romans, that would awaken them from their blindness. For several years of my mission I had hoped that there was some way to demonstrate to them, some argument that could come up from the Christ mind that would convince them. That is why I engaged with the scribes and Pharisees.

I thought somehow there must be an ultimate argument that will convince these people and help them see how they are out of alignment with the reality that I see through the Christ mind. But you see, the Christ mind has no ultimate argument against the mind of anti-christ, for in the mind of anti-christ there is no ultimate argument. When you are in the mind of anti-christ you think that you are God. You think that your definition of good and evil is the ultimate one. As long as you uphold that definition, you can disprove any Christed being who tries to reason with you. You can even disprove an ascended master for you think you know better than the ascended masters.

This is the condition of those who are the most trapped in the fallen mind. Your arguments have no effect on them whatsoever. They have no truth in them wherewith the truth of your words can resonate. There is no resonance in them for they have killed truth, they have killed Christ in themselves, thinking they are actually elevated to a superior status.

My beloved, this is what I finally realized shortly before my arrest and trial, and that is why I stood there and did not defend myself. What would have been the outcome of me defending myself? They would only have mocked me and rejected anything that could be said.

Even though I knew that they would execute me, I still thought that until the very end God would send angels to rescue me and demonstrate that a Christed being can win over the fallen beings even here in the physical. I thought that God would show an undeniable sign so that those who killed the

Christ cannot fail to see what they have done. Again, there is no undeniable sign.

Who is it that needs to change?

Even God and his angels cannot show an undeniable sign for the fallen consciousness can, as I have explained, deny anything. This I did not realize until I was hanging on the cross where I was expecting that I would be rescued by angels. Then it suddenly dawned on me that it was not the fallen ones who needed to change; it was *I* who needed to change.

The fallen ones, what they did to me was in a sense inconsequential because there was never an opportunity that those who were the most blind among them would be awakened. There was a certain opportunity that those that I had taken on as my disciples could be awakened, for they were not as trapped in the fallen consciousness as the Sanhedrin and the Roman leaders. Nevertheless, those who are the most trapped cannot be awakened by anything that you might say or that you might demonstrate. I came to the realization while I was hanging, feeling the weight of my body threatening to suffocate me, feeling the intense pain of having so much of my body weight hanging on the nails in my hands, feeling how my lungs were filling up so that I could barely breathe, knowing that it was just a matter of minutes before my physical body would expire.

As I was hanging there, I finally saw that the crucifixion and my entire mission was never about changing the fallen beings. It was about changing my own attitude and outlook so that I could make the decision to be completely non-attached to the fallen beings and to leave them behind. I needed to be willing to leave them behind completely and utterly, to be willing to let God and God's law take command of what should happen or should not happen to them. I was finally non-attached to their fate, to their destiny. It was no longer my responsibility to do anything with or for the fallen beings.

Your personal cross

This is one of the last initiations you must pass on earth. It often takes an individual form, for as Venus said, you descend with a certain vision that you want to improve things on earth. You want to produce a certain result, and that vision is your personal cross. The vision that you need to do something that depends on the choices of other people, especially those in the fallen consciousness, that vision, that belief, becomes your personal cross.

You will be hanging on it until you see this and until you desire to do what I did: Give up the last ghost, give up that last spirit that you created when you experienced the initial shock of taking embodiment on earth. When you experienced that you came here with the best of intentions, but that you were viciously attacked, ridiculed and mocked by the fallen beings. At that moment, you created a spirit to deal with this, and ever since then, your life has revolved around trying to give that spirit the outcome that is defined by the matrix, the thought matrix, that created the spirit.

It can never happen, my beloved. You can, as Venus explained, help raise the earth by becoming an open door for love, but you cannot help raise the earth if you hold in your mind a fixed, physical outcome. This is what you need to let go of. There are many, many spiritual people on earth today – the 10,000 with the potential to manifest Christhood but millions more who can manifest some degree of Christhood – that are precisely in the situation that they still hold the image that they can change someone else. Let go of it, my beloved, and focus on changing yourself so that you win your complete freedom of non-attachment to the choices of other self-aware beings. Do you see what I am trying to explain to you here?

There are phases of the spiritual path. There is indeed a phase where you need to awaken from the mass consciousness. In order to awaken yourself, you realize what is the problem on earth and you realize the need that someone must seek to raise their individual consciousness and the collective. Some-one must take a stand. Someone must do something. That is why the Christ went out and ministered to the people. There is nothing wrong with this. It is a natural phase on the path.

But what I am seeking to help you see here is that it is not necessary for you to maintain the illusion that you are here to save the fallen beings until moments before you exit the phys-ical realm for the last time. You can overcome that illusion earlier, which will only help you actually fulfill your divine plan and the full potential for your Christhood. When you let go of all attachments to other people and to saving specific people who cannot be changed because their minds will reject any-thing you say, anything you show them.

Overcome vanity!

Vanity of vanity, all is vanity. It is vanity to think you can change those in the fallen mindset. Nothing could ever con-vince them. They can he changed from within when they have had enough, but for those who have not had enough there is nothing you can do to change them. As long as you think it is your job to change them, you cannot manifest the fullness of your Christhood, and you cannot help those that you can help, those that *can* be changed.

So many times we see people who are close to manifesting Christhood become attached to helping a specific person or a specific group of people, for they spend their time and energy on this, but they would never have a chance to change these people's minds anyway. In pursuing this impossible goal, they then neglect the fact that there are many people that they could help, there are many people who could be changed for they are open to changing their minds. They simply need some guidance, they need some statement of truth that resonates with the truth in their hearts.

I am not saying you have been wrong for seeking to work with the fallen beings. In many cases they have deserved an opportunity, and thus it was right for you to be in a relationship with them for a time. But I am saying that there does come a point where you need to recognize that cycles have turned and now it is time to just transcend that fallen consciousness so it has nothing in you—so that the prince of this world, in whatever form he might appear, has nothing in you. This is what I desire you to ponder at this Easter in 2013.

The next years give great opportunities for the spiritual people on earth to increase their creative momentum on the seven rays. This dispensation that has been started by the Chohans is a major dispensation for this planet. I am sure you are at some level of your being realizing that the many problems you see on earth can only be solved through creative vision. [This dispensation is explained in a series of books with the series title *The Path of Self-Mastery*. The first book is *The Power of Self*.]

Unlocking your creativity

You cannot continue to do what you have always done and expect to have different results. You must find creative solutions, and that can happen only by increasing your momentum on the seven rays. I am in no way telling you not to be creative. I am simply telling you: Direct your creativity where it has the most opportunity to produce results. I had a special mission 2,000 years ago to bring judgment to a particular group of fallen beings. I did so by interacting with them and by letting them execute me. In today's Aquarian age, the fallen beings are no longer the primary goal for the Christed ones in embodiment, neither to rescue them nor to judge them. The primary goal is to express your creativity – the Divine Creativity from your I AM Presence – to bring forth creative solutions to the many problems that are crying out for solution.

So much is already happening in many fields of life. Such creativity is already beginning to be expressed that surely many of the problems that today seem to have no solution will be solved within a surprisingly short time span. I simply admonish you this: Stop seeking to change those who cannot be changed. Focus your attention and energy on bringing forth creative solutions for those who can and will transcend the human sense of self, those who can and will be spiritually reborn and thereby transcend the consciousness of death.

Let go of that spirit that is focused on changing or saving or judging the spirits of the fallen beings. It is simply spirit fighting spirit and it can never lead to a decisive outcome. When the Christ is born in your heart, and when you help inspire others to let the Christ be born in their hearts, then there is a decisive outcome and the earth moves closer to the ascension point. This is how to use your focus, your energies, your attention.

Let a word to the wise be sufficient, for I am not concerned at all about seeking to reach those who have proven that they cannot be reached. Let them pass from the screen of life on earth according to cosmic law that never fails.

I wish you, my beloved, a Happy Easter. I wish you the happiness that you can never experience when you are attached to those in the fallen consciousness. They do not know what happiness is, and when you experience and express it, they see it as a threat. Be not concerned about this. Allow yourself to be truly happy for the fact that you know Christ within your heart. Knowing the inner Christ is the key to happiness. I say again: "Happy Easter."

About the Author

Kim Michaels is an accomplished writer and author. He has conducted spiritual conferences and workshops in 14 countries, has counseled hundreds of spiritual students and has done numerous radio shows on spiritual topics. Kim has been on the spiritual path since 1976. He has studied a wide variety of spiritual teachings and practiced many techniques for raising consciousness. Since 2002 he has served as a messenger for Jesus and other ascended masters. He has brought forth extensive teachings about the mystical path, many of them available for free on his websites: *www.askrealjesus.com*, *www.ascendedmasteranswers.com*, *www.ascendedmasterlight.com* and *www.transcendencetoolbox.com*. For personal information, visit Kim at *www.KimMichaels.info*.

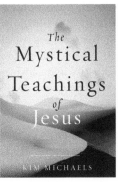

The teachings in this book have helped hundreds of thousands of people gain a deeper appreciation for Jesus's teachings about the mystical path that he taught 2,000 years ago and that he still teaches today—for those who are able to make an inner connection with him.

TODAY MANY PEOPLE CANNOT find a lasting heart connection to the real Jesus and his teachings because, according to most Christian churches, Jesus no longer talks to us. In reality, Jesus is a spiritual being and he is working to help all people who are able to raise their consciousness and attune to his Presence. For the past 2,000 years he has maintained a line of communication through those who have been willing to serve as messengers for his Living Word and who have pursued an understanding of his true message instead of settling for official Christian doctrines.

In this book, the ascended Jesus reveals the mystical teachings that he gave to his most advanced disciples. He explains why his true teachings are as relevant today as they were two millennia ago and how you can develop a personal relationship with him— one of the most remarkable spiritual teachers of all time.

Once you admit that mainstream religious traditions have not answered your questions about life, it is truly liberating to read the deep and meaningful answers in this book. Encouraging, moving and profound, this enlightening book will help you attain inner attunement with Jesus, even mystical union with him.

You will learn how to:
- recognize the silent, inner voice of Christ in your heart
- achieve permanent inner peace and happiness by getting connected with the Christ Consciousness
- heal yourself from emotional wounds
- get guidance from Jesus, who is your greatest teacher and friend
- communicate directly with Jesus

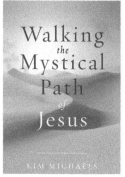

The teachings in this book have helped hundreds of thousands of people gain a deeper appreciation for the mystical path that Jesus taught to his disciples 2000 years ago, the path towards union with God, a state of mind beyond most people's highest dreams.

TODAY MANY PEOPLE HAVE trouble discovering the small, easy and practical steps towards a state of consciousness that is beyond human conflicts and pitfalls. In this book the ascended master Jesus describes how to start walking the mystical path that will eventually restore our most natural ability: the direct experience of God within ourselves.

This book empowers you to discover your personal path and make steady progress towards peace of mind and an inner, mystical experience of God.

Inspiring and profound, this enlightening book contains questions and answers that are easy to read and that help you walk the mystical path of Jesus.

You will learn how to:

- Use the cosmic mirror to speed up your growth
- Get out of old reactionary patterns
- Become free from difficult situations and guilt
- Control your mind
- Leave behind a painful past
- Open your heart to the flow of love from within
- Heal the wounds in your psychology

Hundreds of thousands of people have been inspired and uplifted by the profound teachings released in the form of conversations between the ascended master Jesus and Kim Michaels.

IN THIS BOOK JESUS DESCRIBES in a very personal way the more advanced stages of the mystical or spiritual path. Jesus describes through practical examples how our souls get fragmented in different embodiments and how the pieces of the soul get lost when we have experienced deep traumas in this lifetime or during previous lifetimes. The result is that our souls become vulnerable to different soul diseases that reduce our ability to enjoy life fully. Jesus explains how to restore our most natural ability—the ability to communicate with God directly. He skillfully explains how to make completely free choices in a world that seems to be full of toxic emotions and attitudes: fear, pride and guilt. Jesus explains how to overcome the sharpest tool of the dualistic mind—doubt combined with fear and pride.

In an easy to read question and answer form, Jesus guides you to a deeper understanding of how some lifestreams are young and mature, some rebel against God and some seek union with God. He helps you break through the opposition from both outside forces and the inner enemy of the ego.

You will learn how to:
- make use of your closest spiritual teacher – Jesus – on your own mystical path
- turn your past traumatic soul experiences into a forward step
- restore the fragments of your soul and by doing this developing your own direct union with God
- learn from even false teachers and overcome fear, pride and doubt
- avoid being disappointed by spiritual organizations
- create a new identity based on love

Freedom
from
Ego
Illusions

One of the most remarkable spiritual teachers known to humankind is Jesus who taught the mystical path of reunion with God to his disciples 2,000 years ago. Today, Jesus, as an ascended master, teaches that same path to those who are willing to be his modern disciples. Jesus knows that the major obstacle we all face on the mystical journey is the human ego.

THE EGO IS THE MOST SUBTLE CHALLENGE on the spiritual path because it distorts our thoughts, emotions, attitudes, even the way we look at life. In this book Jesus offers his most loving guidance in order to help you rise beyond the level of consciousness affected by the ego. In this new-found freedom, you will be able to grasp the divine vision, both for yourself and for the world you create.

Jesus teaches you how to start seeing through the illusions that the ego uses to keep you trapped in a lower state of consciousness. You will learn:

- How to avoid having your life consumed by an impossible quest
- How to distinguish between the ego itself and its illusions
- How the world view of the ego becomes a self-fulfilling prophecy
- How to rise above the black-and-white thinking of the ego
- How to avoid being trapped in the gray thinking of the ego
- How the ego can use a spiritual teaching to stop your growth
- How to overcome internal divisions that sabotage your growth

You will also find an in-depth discussion about why and how the ego was created. You will learn that you will always have an element of ego as long as you are in embodiment, but that you can come to see through the ego and make creative decisions.

A comprehensive guide to how you can avoid wasting your life on the fruitless games played by the human ego

TODAY MANY PEOPLE are trapped within tight boundaries defined by the ego games—the games of survival, security, power, control, competition, validation, responsibility and blame. With penetrating insight, the ascended master Jesus teaches that on our spiritual journey the human ego plays games that are very similar to the ones played by Frankenstein's monster: "The story of Doctor Frankenstein was inspired by the ascended masters in order to illustrate one of the fundamental properties of the ego. The plot is simple, namely that a doctor – with seemingly benign motives – stitches together dead body parts and infuses them with life. Once the creature has received a form of life, it displays a survival instinct that makes it willing to kill anyone standing in its way, even its own creator."

Jesus teaches through practical steps that spiritual rebirth requires us to voluntarily and consciously – if it is not conscious, it cannot be voluntary – let the old human identity die and accept that we are reborn into a higher spiritual sense of identity. You will learn how to:

- make LIFE decisions that turn your life experience positive
- recognize the ego games and the illusions that hold back your personal growth
- avoid having your life consumed by the ego's quest for security
- overcome the ego's survival, control, validation, blame and competition games and find true validation from your spiritual self
- take responsibility for yourself and stop feeling responsible for other people

"A person who controls the world is still inferior to one who controls his or her own mind. True personal power means that in any situation you encounter on earth, you can choose your reaction freely. Instead of reacting through one of the games of the ego, you can react by being the open door for your I AM Presence and the power of God." – JESUS